PRAISE FOR *AMERICAN GOULASH*

"Talk about growing up in a pressure cooker! A poignant recipe for laughter and tears."

—Gene (E.C.) Ayres, writer for
The Smurfs and *Dennis the Menace*

"The bad thing about *American Goulash* is that you wish Stephanie Yuhas was sitting with you over coffee sharing these stories. Reading it is the next best thing. If you feel like an outsider, she is here to tell you in her touching and funny memoir that you're not alone. Yuhas is a wonderful storyteller."

—Mary Jo Pehl, actress/writer for
Mystery Science Theater 3000

"*American Goulash* is a thoughtful and entertaining depiction of a first-generation American living amidst old-world sensibilities. With poise, intellect, and unrelenting cheer, Stephanie Yuhas paints negative life events into engaging life lessons. If you wonder how this young lady can be so well adjusted, remember that diamonds are born under pressure."

—David Conant, executive director
of WRTI public radio

"It's funny, sentimental, and just an all-around great read!"

—David Goodman, writer/reviewer
for *Geekadelphia*

"What the hell is goulash?"

—James Rolfe, actor/director for
Angry Video Game Nerd

AMERICAN GOULASH

STORIES FROM THE MELTING POT

STEPHANIE YUHAS

Booktrope Editions
Seattle, WA 2014

Cover Design by Stephanie Yuhas
Digital Assets by Chris Potako & Pete Lauritzen
Edited by Kathy Harding

This is a creative work of non-fiction. Events, locales, and conversations have been recreated from the author's memories of them, but some names, places, and identifying details have been changed to protect the privacy of the individuals mentioned.

PRINT ISBN 978-1-93596-173-4

EPUB ISBN 978-1-62015-077-1

Library of Congress Control Number: 2014917989

To Anyu,

I love you.

Don't read this, OK? Let's go get ice cream instead. Any flavor but vanilla.

Vanilla sucks.

INTRODUCTION:
HISTORY MAKES MYSTERY

WHETHER I'M DANCING with my shopping cart at the grocery store or harassing wallflowers at networking events with kitschy icebreakers, these days I'm a tornado of positivity that baffles, annoys, and occasionally amuses onlookers.

I was not always this way. I used to be the brooding, self-conscious foreigner doodling in the back of the classroom. Then one day it dawned on me that the only reason I exist is because of toilet paper, coffee liqueur, and Soviet oppression. How can anybody with that unlikely an existence really have anything other than an absurd appreciation for life and the oddness that comes with it?

I realize this contradiction warrants some backstory. It's difficult and uncomfortable to mention something as horrific and un-funny as war in a comedy memoir about growing up as a modern American amongst old-world sensibilities. Out of respect for my family and my culture, I wanted to put this story into some historical context. It's both fascinating and horrific, like seeing how much puss you can squeeze out of a pimple.

Much of my family's immigration story has been shrouded in mystery, like a secret recipe someone took to their grave. Whenever I ask the family elders about our history, they change the subject. I'm not sure if they're hiding something, trying not to relive the past, or simply not paying attention because they're too busy trying to get me to eat more blood. (More on that later.)

I can't say I blame my family for their silence. In the Eastern Bloc, they learned how to keep their heads down and how to change the subject through cascades of non sequiturs. I've had to cobble my family history together through leading questions and booze.

Legend has it that my grandmother, Nagymama, was born in Yugoslavia in 1911 and immigrated to Transylvania during World War II with her sister, Felecia. She smuggled black market toiletries to the citizens of Saint George, a primarily ethnically Hungarian region within Romania. Nagymama made enough money through sales of her embroidered linens and smuggled goods to purchase a two-room house. She was satisfied with her single life as a sketchy entrepreneur and enjoyed tending to her immaculate vegetable and rose gardens.

Nagymama attended the Mona Lisa School of Smiling.

Around 1950, the occupying Soviets informed Nagymama that because she had no husband or children she had to let soldiers board in her spare room. She feared what would happen if she boarded a strange man that had legal authority over her, so later that day she proposed marriage to her gas man, Zoltan. He declined on the basis that they'd only met a few times, he was twelve years younger than she was, and he was already in a loving relationship with a beautiful woman.

Historically, Nagymama has never been the type to take no for an answer. She went to the central market, met up with Zoltan's mother, and offered her black market wares—specifically, luxurious, one-ply toilet paper—in exchange for her son's hand in marriage. Believing Nagymama to be rich, Zoltan's mother pimped out her only son.

They all moved into the two-room house. No love ever bloomed between Nagymama and Zoltan. Their relationship remained a business transaction and life insurance policy. They each recognized the value of having kids who'd take care of them when they grew old. Their merger produced a daughter, my aunt Neni.

After Nagymama became pregnant with their second child (my mother), Zoltan became paranoid. Nagymama was growing colder and more critical and he was getting odd fevers and chills. He told everyone in the village that Nagymama was poisoning him. No one believed him, teasing that a mouse of a woman like Nagymama could never take down a seven-foot-tall pylon like Zoltan.

One night, while Nagymama had her back turned to prepare gulyásleves, Zoltan attempted to stab her. Zoltan's mother saw him lunge and pushed him over. The knife missed Nagymama by a few inches. Unfazed, Nagymama invited the Soviet authorities over for dinner and left the knife in the floorboard to prove that her life was in danger. Only then was Nagymama legally allowed to both file for divorce and keep her second room soldier-free.

Zoltan received no punishment for trying to murder Nagymama. It was apparently not an uncommon scenario. Zoltan signed papers to emancipate his children and was delighted to pursue his passion for fishing. Presumably, he was also able to eat without being concerned that his wife was secretly poisoning him. (On a related note, I often overheard Nagymama muttering in her sleep, like a character delivering a Shakespearean soliloquy, about poisoning some man. So maybe he wasn't so paranoid after all.)

Nagymama and her two daughters lived together until they received a letter from the government in the late '60s. Their house was being seized and turned into a parking lot. Neni applied for and won a lottery to go work at a sweatshop in the United States. When the letter arrived, Nagymama hid it in a couch cushion. Her daughters found it and confronted her only days before the house was to be taken.

Nagymama thought she could convince the Soviets to let her keep her house if she stayed inside it when the bulldozers came. She was more comfortable living as a bootlegger under an oppressive regime than facing the prospect of an uncertain future in a country where she did not speak the language, couldn't drive, and didn't have black market connections. Her daughters did not feel the same way. My mother vowed to take care of Nagymama until she died in exchange for freedom from Soviet rule. In 1970, they boarded a boat, came to New Jersey, and never looked back.

They used what little money they had to buy a small house and rented out the spare room to tenants from the Hungarian newspaper. One night my mother had some Kahlua with one of these tenants. One thing led to another. She thought she was barren. He told her he'd had a vasectomy. She was wrong; he lied.

At the clinic, my mother realized she shared Nagymama's desire for an insurance policy—someone to take care of her when *she* was old. She used the money Nagymama gave her for the abortion to buy baggy clothing to hide the pregnancy. When my father realized she was still with child, he married her to "preserve the Hungarian honor." They were divorced before I turned two.

It was a crappy situation for everyone—and not because my family history starts with a toilet paper dowry. My family tree might be missing a lot of branches, but the few twigs of information that I've gathered have affected my entire outlook on life. Who we are is partially a reflection of our experiences. I've been fortunate to live a life of relative freedom as a result of the daily struggles and the sacrifices of my ancestors. I have a deep sense of joy—perhaps a sometimes aggressive bubbliness—because I appreciate how unlikely the butterfly effect leading to my existence actually was.

I'll never be a true Hungarian, the same way I'll never be a true American. I'm a far cry from the cauldrons of gulyásleves that brought comfort to countless herdsmen in the Great Hungarian Plain, and I'll always be a cheap imitation of the name-brand Hamburger Helper. I'm a hodgepodge, a messy bowl of American Goulash, a side dish in the melting pot that is New Jersey.

From this point on, all I can tell is my true story from my blended cultural perspective. I've changed some of the names and places so I don't hurt or boost people's egos. People's egos should stay exactly where they are. I did not write this book as an official representation of any culture, ethnicity, neighborhood in New Jersey, etc. Please do not make me an official representative of anything; I am a terrible salesperson. This is simply a retelling of my childhood stories, sprinkled with my particular off-brand of paprika.

Bon Appétit! Jó étvágyat! I hope you enjoy!

I promise, the rest of this is funny.

CHAPTER 1: YAK PUKE

I SPENT the first sixteen years of my life sleeping on a piece of upholstery foam in the living room of a 425-square-foot shack in the middle of suburban New Jersey. My roommate in this dilapidated estate was Nagymama, my old-world Grandma, a cube of a woman standing 4 feet tall, 4 feet wide, and 4 feet deep. She was so astoundingly symmetrical that I sometimes imagined she was a human matryoshka nesting doll and wondered if there might be other smaller Nagymamas nestled inside of her.

My mother, Anyu, purchased the shack as a severely discounted starter home, hoping that she would find her American Dream—a husband with a better house. After a cancelled engagement, two failed marriages, and an unplanned pregnancy (me!), she settled into the home with Nagymama and permanently made peace with the squalor. Despite the above, my surroundings were not crummy enough to elicit any of the following: a full scholarship to college, a booking from Oprah, or any sympathy from my immediate or extended family. I knew from their stories that they'd endured far worse conditions back in Transylvania, an actual real place often thought to be fictional thanks to Mr. Bram Stoker.

My family immigrated in 1970 to Piscataway (pronounced "Piss-the-cat-away" by local children and immature adults). Piscataway is located in Central Jersey, another mythical area no one from outside of the region believes to exist. This is because in conversation, New Jersey is almost always broadly divided into two sections. The first, South Jersey, is basically Philadelphia, but with no left turns, way more strip malls, and cheap gas you're not legally permitted to pump yourself. North Jersey, a.k.a. New York, Jr., is stereotyped in pop culture as the land of big-haired, fake-tanned, gum-chewing girls with Fran Drescher accents. I've never met anyone who fits that description. Perhaps they're legends, like the Jersey

Devil, but more orange. Or maybe I haven't seen any of these delightful creatures because Central Jersey is in fact a real place, a "third half," with its own quirky culture and issues.

**Paper plates. Voted Most Amusing Toy
for Kids since 1904.**

Long before I was born, Central Jersey was primarily farmland, giving New Jersey its nickname: "The Garden State" (and its slogan "I got yer tomatas right 'ere!"). These days it's filled with a culturally diverse group of stressed-out commuters and healthcare workers, all of whom pay high property taxes and are tired of hearing questions like, "Do you know any of *The Sopranos*?" or "Are you friends with Snookie?"

The streets of Piscataway in the 1980s were littered with newly built cookie-cutter bi-levels, identical except for their alternating shades of Easter-colored vinyl siding. My family's home was the black sheep of the neighborhood. Although the other homes faced the street, our house faced the neighbor, like the creepy guy on a subway who stares at his fellow passengers in the ear. Driving down the property value of the neighborhood was our hobby. When the siding on the house began to mold and oxidize, Nagymama painted the surrounding plaster, doors, and windows the perfect color to match the decay. Every season, she rifled through the discontinued paint section of the hardware store, determined to find the ugliest shade of green. It was somewhere between an old school DOS prompt and the blank screen of a first-generation Game Boy.

I looked forward to these trips because it meant that I could drag Anyu to look at the wondrous rolls of Pink Panther-brand cotton candy. Every time I reached for them, she slapped my hand away and told me I would die if I ate it. I told her she was mean. Looking back on it, other customers must have been confused about why a three-year-old would be demanding to buy a deadly, deadly thirty-nine-foot roll of PINK Fiberglass Insulation.

During her multi-week painting marathons, Nagymama would mix oil colors with acrylics and despair into a chunky tapestry that could only be referred to as "Yak Puke Green." I always wanted to help, so Nagymama would hand me a roller and instantly scale the house like a 75-year-old Gypsy Spiderman. I'd unhelpfully apply dozens of layers of paint to the only corner I could reach.

When Anyu got around to noticing that Nagymama was subjecting a toddler to fume-filled manual labor, she'd take me inside and tell me: "Don't go outside. You'll get freckles. And then no one vill love you." This ingrained itself into my psyche until age 30, when my doctor told me I had a severe vitamin D deficiency and would get rickets if I continued to cover myself with SPF 90+ sunscreen.

I never protested when my mother called me inside. Because I was taught the outside world contained dangers (the sun, snakes, and the mailman), I embraced the safer adventures of the inside world. To a small child, the four rooms of our home seemed huge. There was my mother's peach bedroom, the blue kitchen, a single pink bathroom, and the chaotic multi-colored living room/dining room/bedroom/family room/occasional bathroom that Nagymama and I shared (hereinafter referred to as "The Room").

The Room had wall-to-wall carpeting that was covered in a second layer of mismatched remnant squares for protection. So much was made of maintaining the cleanliness of the wall-to-wall carpet that I spent my childhood jumping between carpet squares as if the real carpet was hot lava. On the rare occasion we had guests, Anyu would hide the carpet squares to reveal perfect patches of clean carpeting lined with deep rivers of stains.

The decor was a cross between Soviet barracks and an American college dorm. Between ancient floral doilies hung our sole painting, a boat. Nagymama had lifted it from a Howard Johnson's where she worked as a cleaning lady and painted the wooden frame gold in order to make it more valuable. She cut out pictures of commemorative Jesus plates and taped them to the other wall, like a 2-D simulacrum of the china cabinet she wished she had. On special occasions, Nagymama let me browse through magazines with her and cut out a picture of a plate I liked. We'd tape my picture to the wall next to her pictures, where it would remain for a day or two until she decided the Starship Enterprise clashed with Noah's Ark. Its five-year mission to explore strange new worlds unceremoniously ended in the grimy garbage can, next to a half dozen mouse traps. Finally, between the china cabinet and Nagymama's bed, hung the pièce de résistance, a leather canteen of holy water (just in case).

My mother's bedroom was also decorated with cutouts. Like a teenage fangirl, she taped up tabloid photos of Elvis and old 1970s calendars of male bathing suit models.

"I pray to God dat a sexy man vill show up on our doorstep someday," she would say to a mostly naked Burt Reynolds, who I learned as an adult is a different person from Tom Selleck. They were, and are, all chest hair and mustaches to me.

The only way that any man, let alone a sexy mustache man, could get to our door would be if he dropped out of the sky. Our house sat on a quarter acre of property covered by so many dead trees and branches that even the royal prince from *Sleeping Beauty* would have trouble bursting through the pointy mess on his mighty steed. The entire property was surrounded by a green wire fence, which we lovingly referred to as The Kapu ("gate" in Hungarian). We had no pets, so The Kapu was our guard dog and referred to as such.

"Stephie, did you lock The Kapu? It protects our fortress! Look at The Kapu and make sure no burglars are trying to get in. Stephie, did you remember to walk and feed The Kapu?"

The Kapu remained locked at all times despite the fact that we had nothing in our home worth stealing. Nagymama was the only one who possessed keys to The Kapu. One she kept in an old blue tin box that used to hold Danish sugar cookies, and the other she hid in the pocket of an old robe, way in the back of the closet behind many pointy things. After this book is published, The Kapu keys will likely move to another location, like the island in *Lost*, to ensure that no one else knows this secret.

Getting in and out of the house has been an issue my whole life because of The Kapu. Anyu said it was there to protect us from crazy psycho killers. The way I see it, crazy psycho killers are probably good at three things: psycho killing, gym class, and hopping fences. Why bother?

As a result of the combination of the hideousness of my childhood home, our strong Count Chocula accents, and Nagymama's hobby of chasing creatures and people with a broom, the children in the neighborood started a rumor that we were witches. I can't blame them.

Nagymama specifically requested that we take her photo in a graveyard. To enhance the legend, I guess.

Nagymama's skin was so translucent it looked as if her entire body was covered in a fine layer of white powder, including her eyes, which were a milky gray color. She meticulously curled and dyed her chin-length hair into a powdered-wig-like formation. In cold weather, she donned a white hat that resembled a failed laboratory mating of a *Gilligan Island*'s sailor cap with a colonial tricorn hat. Her winter coat was a chain-embellished, military-style, hounds tooth blazer with enormous shoulder pads (bought on sale, 90 percent off, from Joyce Leslie, circa 1984). Viewed from a distance, anyone could have mistaken Nagymama for the ghost of Revolutionary War hero George Washington, patrolling our yard for Redcoats.

When Nagymama wasn't unintentionally posing for famous paintings where she crossed the Delaware, she donned a babushka with curlers underneath, a housecoat, and decrepit slippers—her papucs—which were more duct tape than footwear.

She was deathly afraid of taking her papucs off, citing the fact that bare feet could lead to ailments ranging anywhere from fungus to pneumonia to pregnancy. (I literally thought that babies were born out of your feet, but more on that later.) For the sake of general health and well-being, Anyu and I were also forced to wear papucs at all times. If we didn't, Nagymama would scream "Papucs!" at the top of her lungs while slapping our feet with a fakanál, (pronounced Fuck-A-Nahl, Hungarian for "word that sounds dirty in English but really means wooden spoon.") The fakanál was used as a combination gavel, semaphore flag, and whipping rod. It also worked for stirring things on occasion.

No matter how many papucs Anyu bought her, Nagymama would wear the oldest, nastiest pair. Nagymama would staple, glue, sew, and tape these slippers until they were nothing but a single piece of cardboard attached to each foot. Lack of proper footwear did not stop Nagymama from performing her daily death-defying chores: fending off neighborhood dogs, nailing splintery planks of wood to things, and sweeping the roof.

Between Nagymama and me, Anyu had two toddlers to look after constantly. As a child, I did not understand why Anyu always looked concerned or why she was always wringing her hands. I assumed she was unhappy because of Nagymama. Nagymama was our boss, our leader, the commander in chief who barked orders. Anyu always went easy on me. She was my buddy, more like a big sister than a mother, and I liked her. On days when Nagymama was at work or visiting a family member, Anyu and I had playtime together. Without Nagymama's critical eye over her shoulder, Anyu was able to read me Berenstain Bears stories and feed me endless McDonald's Happy Meals.

I assumed that Nagymama was the enemy. But when Nagymama and Anyu started fighting almost exclusively about me, I realized that Anyu was unhappy because I existed. I wanted to make her happy because I was afraid she was going to leave me if I didn't, just like my father had. I drew a picture of us walking on a rainbow.

"Is this how ugly you think I am?" she frowned.

I found Anyu to be beautiful; I just sucked at drawing at age four. I'd tried to depict her big blue-gray eyes. They were so much better than mine, which I'd drawn as small, ugly, poo-brown dots. She also had pretty, long, permed hair like all of the 1980s television stars I admired. My haircut made me look like a boy.

"I used to be beautiful," she continued, pointing to a detailed sketch that hung behind her bed. Her first husband had commissioned it from a boardwalk artist in San Francisco. She had been 18, new in America, enjoying a whirlwind romance with a Romanian named Tibor. She was only married to him for two weeks before Nagymama guilted her into coming back home to New Jersey from the West Coast. Tibor refused to live with Nagymama. I was never sure how Anyu felt about Tibor after their breakup, but the porcelain Lladro statue and portrait he gave her were prized possessions, symbols of a time when she felt desirable. I might not have understood her self-esteem issues, but I understood that no picture of mine was going on the fridge until I could accurately replicate the boardwalk drawing. I decided to get better at drawing so I could make Anyu happy.

Until I became a better artist, I had to find other ways to make Anyu happy. I heard her laugh at a word her sister, Neni, said once. I didn't know what it meant. I practiced saying it to myself until I was confident that I knew how to say it. While Anyu was plucking her eyebrows one day, I burst into the bathroom and proudly said, "Fuck!" as loud as I could. She gasped. She didn't need to punish me; I knew from her expression that I'd done something wrong and I was a failure. In reality, part of the reason she'd had such a horrified expression was because she'd accidentally plucked off half of her eyebrow arch as a result of my language, giving herself a quizzical look. Her eyebrows grew back in three weeks, but I didn't say that word again for many, many years. I decided to stick to drawing.

CHAPTER 2: THE OTHER PARENT

NAGYMAMA WAS ON the roof again.

For the first few years of my life, Anyu did keypunch and assembly line work at Johnson & Johnson. This left me with my other parent, the black-and-white Zenith television we kept in the middle of the room. It was the only television in the house, if you didn't count the other larger, broken television upon which it was precariously perched. It had a sixteen-inch screen, weighed ten tons, and had no remote control. Instead of buttons, it had two knobs: volume and channel. Any time I wanted to change the channel, I had to use all of my might to wrench the knob with a pair of pliers that were embedded in it. No one saw any danger in leaving pliers around electronics and a small child.

This television was my prized possession. I spent almost every waking moment watching one of the four network channels that came in clearly. I didn't understand what anyone was saying on the screen because we only spoke Hungarian around the house. I mostly watched television so I could draw pictures of the actors on the back of placemats that Nagymama brought home from Howard Johnson's. She provided me with an unlimited amount of these placemats and the standard four-pack of crayons that came with them. I always found an opportunity, however, to make secret drawings of my favorite characters on the tiny part of the wall behind my nursery dresser, a wooden monstrosity decorated with the painted picture of an oddly sultry bunny rabbit. Anyu or Nagymama usually found these drawings, got mad, and took away my crayons, at which point I'd go back to my second favorite thing to do: playing in front of the television with Barbie.

I had a bunch of ratty Barbies that had been passed down to me from my cousins Erin and Irina, who were already tweens at the time. I had a sack of about a dozen of them, including memorable favorites like

Paraplegic Barbie™, Headless Barbie™, and Barbie That is Only a Head™. It wasn't until 1985 that I saw a commercial for Dream Glow Barbie.

A Barbie with all her parts that glows in the dark? To a three-year-old child, glow-in-the-dark paint exists at a level of mysticism on par with fairy godmothers, unicorns, and my cousins' goldfish that seemed to have the power of resurrection because I had seen it die in front of me twice.

Dream Glow Barbie? Check. Short shorts? Check. Fly catcher? Check.

I talked about this Barbie every single day until Santa bought it for me the next year, when it was old news and on the clearance rack. I cherished this doll and carried her to bed with me to absorb her radioactive goodness. I even saved the box she came in because I'd never had an official Barbie box. I memorized every detail of that box and treasured it because it gave me precious insight into the world of Barbie. Apparently, she had a boyfriend named Ken and a sister named Skipper, and she could interact with alternate dimensions where she had different color hair or skin but was still somehow Barbie.

I also discovered that deep inside of the box, past the stabby wires holding Barbie in place, there was a tiny catalogue, featuring assorted Barbie clothes and shoes. None of the items interested me because my other Barbie dolls had some sort of physical deformity that fashion could not fix, and there was no outfit Dream Glow Barbie could possibly get that was as awesome as her star-filled pink ball gown. But when I unfolded the catalogue, there was a poster on the back for the greatest thing my childhood brain had ever seen: the Barbie Glamour Home.

I begged Anyu to buy it for me for my fifth birthday, but she said it cost more than she and Nagymama made in a week and we'd never be able to afford it. Not understanding what money was, I told them they were mean.

"Ask your asshole father to buy it for you. He can take it out of the child support he never pays," she muttered to herself. Still not understanding what money was, I told her she was mean.

My mother and father had gotten divorced when I was a baby, after a combination of living with an overbearing mother-in-law and being overwhelmed with the desire to spend time with prostitutes had proved too much for my father. The state of New Jersey called it "irreconcilable differences." I was too young to remember what he looked like, but I had a few blurry photos and we spoke on the phone every so often. I could never get his widow's peak, deep voice, and thick Hungarian accent out of my head.

One day I saw a tall, handsome man on TV with a Hungarian accent.

"Anyu, is that my Apu?" I asked.

My mother smiled to herself. "Yes, Stephie, your father sure knows how to suck the blood out of everything."

That man, I realized later, was Bela Lugosi as Dracula.

At the time, however, my mother's comment made perfect sense. We were Transylvanian and my father was never home! From that point on, I thought that Dracula, and vampires and bats in all iterations, were my father, deep inside the television, there to entertain and delight me.

"Apu, I want a Barbie Glamour House!" I screamed at Grandpa from *The Munsters*.

"Apu, can I please have the Working Shower Add-On?" I asked The Count from *Sesame Street*.

"And maybe a Ken doll so Barbie can go on a date?" I begged of Adam West as *Batman*.

No matter how much I begged my TV dads for it, Barbie Glamour Home never came. I thought the television was broken and my father couldn't hear me. I noticed on commercials that sometimes people put coins into a phone to make it work. I found change around the house and started inserting it into the slots of the TV.

This broke the TV. I've never told anyone that I'm the one who broke it. Anyu, if you're reading this, I'd say that you could retroactively ground me for this act, but then again, because I specifically asked you not to read this book, I think I'm absolved of this punishment. Also, you can probably buy yourself a 1974 black-and-white Zenith television with the thirty-seven dollars in change I loaded into the old one. I know you still have it.

After I hammered a quarter into the last remaining speaker of the TV, I had no television and no dollhouse. Sheer boredom forced me to improvise. I found a bunch of cardboard boxes that Nagymama had brought home from the grocery store. By now, my latest crayon punishment was over, and I spent days drawing faux artwork inside the cardboard house and decorating it with scraps of fabric from aunt Neni's upholstery shop. I even managed to use my safety scissors to cut little windows into the side of each box. I used these same safety scissors to make my own Ken, which involved taking my shabbiest Barbie, cutting off her hair, and rubbing her against the driveway for several hours until her boobs were gone, which evidently was the only difference between girls and boys.

Still, I yearned for a Barbie Glamour House, if only for one reason: I wanted Barbie to stand up straight. The cardboard boxes were intended for two-liter bottles of soda; they were about two inches too short for a standard-sized Barbie. Luckily, the Barbies without heads fit fine, and I often played Dinner Party where the headless Barbies would serve decadent plastic meals to seated headed Barbies unable to stand due to the low ceiling. In retrospect, these dinner parties probably looked like a terrifying scene from a Guillermo del Toro film.

Despite the limitations of Barbie's cardboard shanty, I spent a lot of time fabricating elaborate dollhouse structures. Nagymama would spend most of her nights tearing them down. My whole life, Nagymama felt the need to deconstruct and reorganize everything in our house. Nothing I played with was safe. If I turned my back for a moment, my intricate setup of Dominos was in a neat pile. If I used the bathroom, the pegs were removed from my Lite-Brite and filed away by color. She didn't like the pieces that fit into Mr. Potato Head, so she threw them out until all I had was a plastic potato. Because I didn't understand what obsessive-compulsive disorder was, I assumed she was punishing me.

Then one day the phone rang. I always knew it was my father on the phone when the German Shepherd next door would start howling in tune with Anyu's yelling. In my family, there is only one rule to arguing in Hungarian. The loudest always wins.

Apu rarely called, but my fifth birthday was coming up that week.

"He remembered!" I jumped up and down around Anyu's legs.

"Fine, Stephie, talk to your asshole father."

I could hear his mumbled voice protesting from the receiver. I grabbed the heavy mustard-colored rotary phone and struggled to hold it to my ear with both hands.

"Hallo?" I asked shyly.

"Szia, Stephie."

I imagined Bela Lugosi speaking from a coffin phone. "Don't listen to your crazy bitch mother. You know, your name vasn't even supposed to be stupid Stephanie."

"Really, Apu?"

He continued. "Me, I was gonna name you Margitka, proud Magyar name. But she names you some crap outta some American baby name book and tells you you're Transylvanian."

"Apu. . .can I. . .can I. . .have a Barbie Glamour House?"

"Yah, yah. How old you gonna be?"

"Five."

"Okay, fine. I'll get you the Barbie thing for your burstday. But listen, Stefike, you are not to tell anyone that you are a dirty Romanian, you hear me? You are von-hundred-percent Hungarian blood." He coughed and wheezed, a byproduct of his lifetime of smoking. "And any German you have in you from your grandmother, you shit out in your diapers."

"But Apu," I twirled the phone cord around my little foot. "I thought I was from New Jersey."

*   *   *

For the next week, I waited patiently by the window for the UPS truck. My birthday came and went. Every day I jumped up and ran to the door, hoping for that brown truck to burst through the Kapu and bring me a package. After about a month of this, I started to get anxious and asked my mom when the dollhouse Apu promised was coming. Before I knew it, I was hiding in the clothes hamper while Anyu screamed at my father over the phone.

"You have money for booze and vomen but not for your own daughter? This is vhy I don't vant you to talk to her. You make all these promises and then I have to deal with it! Hold on, you tell her yourself. Where the hell did she go?" Anyu pulled the long phone cord over to the hamper and handed it to me. "Your asshole father vants to talk to you."

Apu mumbled a few things into my ear. I burst into tears and hung up the phone.

"Vhat did he say to you?" she asked.

"Apu said that he bought me the Barbie Glamour House and the mailman lost it! He said the mailman probably gave it to another little girl and everyone stole his money so now he can't get me a new one."

Anyu furrowed her brow. "Son of a—"

She sat me down at the kitchen table and grabbed the forbidden crystal glasses from the top of the cupboard.

"Shhh!" she said, winking at me as she filled them to the top with whipped cream. These were Nagymama's special glasses, only to be used when special guests—presumably the Prime Minister of Hungary—came over. The dessert was Reddi-Whip in a fake crystal glass that Nagymama had pilfered from Howard Johnson's. To me it was the most decadent dessert that had ever existed. And I liked sharing a secret with my mom.

Anyu went into the other room and had a phone conversation. I tried to listen in, but she was speaking Romanian, the secret language she never taught me. At home, we primarily spoke Hungarian, but Nagymama and Anyu also spoke Romanian, German, and various old-world pidgin languages used in the villages to trade goats, husbands, or whatever my family had an excess of. I still only knew a few phrases in English, which I'd learned from watching TV, mainly soap operas. We didn't have cable, or my vocabulary would have been a lot more colorful.

About an hour later, Neni showed up to the door, struggling to carry a large square object wrapped in a terrifying clown blanket.

"Stephie, I vant to talk to you," Neni said as she placed the mysterious object on the floor. I cowered because the clown's eyes were watching me. "I know you vant new toys badly, but they are very expensive."

I looked down at the floor and bit my lower lip. Half in sadness, half in clown fear.

"Listen, don't cry. If ve save up our monies, maybe someday you can have many new tings. But for now, I'm going to give you my favorite toy to make it up to you, okay? Happy burstday."

My eyes opened in shock as my aunt unwrapped the blanket to reveal a color television, complete with rabbit ears and a remote. She'd taken her own TV out of her upholstery shop and given it to me. It was dusty, scratched, and a little sticky for some reason, but I didn't care. I didn't even let them take the old TV down before I plugged it into the tangle of brown extension cords that surrounded the room.

"Stephie!" Anyu said with her hands on her hips. "Your aunt brought you a present. Vat do you say to her?"

"Oh my gosh," I exclaimed. "The Smurfs are *blue!*"

CHAPTER 3: BEDTIME

BEDTIME WAS a huge ordeal in my house. There was always a fight because I wanted to stay up and watch TV, especially now that we had it in fuzzy color. And it seemed like my favorite movie, *Splash*, was on all the time. Unfortunately, I don't know how it ends to this day, because it ran thirty minutes over my bedtime.

The only way Anyu could convince me to go to bed was by bribing me with five more minutes of television. This would only happen if I brushed my teeth with a special brand of fun sparkling kids' toothpaste. The fun part came from the fact that it contained as much sugar as a can of orange soda. As a result, I ended up getting cavities in every one of my baby teeth. I may as well have brushed my teeth with Twizzlers. Anyu would then stand there and watch me until I made a bowel movement in the little potty. After whatever I made was analyzed for proper consistency and aroma, I was ushered into bed.

"But you promised, five more minutes of the mermaid movie!"

"No, Nagymama already hid the extension cord, so there's no more TV for tonight."

Then my fit would begin. It was hideous. Thrashing. Crying. After I had expended all of my energy attempting to move a 300-pound television closer to the outlet, Nagymama would lift my exhausted body into bed. No hug, no kiss, no bedtime story. She muttered to herself in a medley of languages while she physically tied me into bed.

Let me explain.

Nagymama was worried that I was going to toss the covers off of myself in the middle of the night, expose my midriff, and catch a "kidney cold," which is a disease Hungarians made up to give themselves something to fret about. To protect me, she would tie the corner of the blanket to the foam mattress with shoelaces. I didn't mind the tying of the blanket. It provided a swaddling effect that comforted me. What bothered me was the feeling of Nagymama's bristly chin hairs scratching my cheek as she reached over me.

After tying me into bed, Nagymama would move every one of the high-backed chairs from the kitchen into the living room and use them to encircle my bed. This was in order to catch me in the event that I untied myself from the blankets and rolled onto my head, thus spilling my disgusting brains on the precious carpet squares. The other ghastly scenario she spoke of included me rolling out of bed, my mother forgetting to secure the front door and Kapu, and me continuing to roll down the street, I guess forever, or until my slumbering frictionless body was picked up by a traveling child organ salesman.

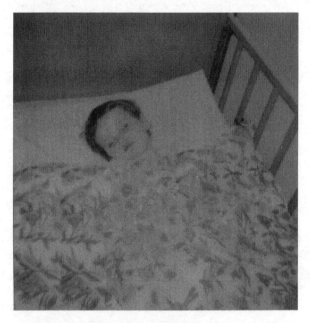

Me, after a long night of drinking.

Every night as I was falling asleep, Nagymama would turn on her flashlight, put on her slippers, grab her hand mirror, walk over to my bed, and put the mirror under my nose. She was checking to make sure I was still alive. I was not just alive but also now awake. Then Nagymama would walk back to her bed and fall right asleep. But I'd remain wide awake. Partially due to Nagymama's loud snoring, partially due to my mother's endless singing of Roy Orbison in the other room:

Pretty voman!
Valking down dah street!
Pretty voman!
Kind of vant some meat!
Pretty vooooman!

When Anyu inevitably came in to check on me as well, she'd be surprised to discover I was awake.

"The house is loud and I'm not tired. More TV?"

Anyu would check to make sure Nagymama was sleeping, then gently unbuckle me from bed and walk me to her room, where the repaired black-and-white Zenith had been moved. I loved watching TV with Anyu because it was one of the few times I had the opportunity to sit in a real bed. It felt like it was a mile in the sky. The bed was tiny so I was able to sit next to Anyu, which is the closest thing we experienced to physical affection. On Saturdays, she'd sneak me out of bed for an extra half hour of *Tales from the Crypt*. I probably shouldn't have been watching a show that scary at my age, but I didn't understand the context and neither did my mom. We both thought it was a comedy. She always called it the *Croochie Froochie* show, which is Hungarian for. . .nothing! I guess she'd made a loose portmanteau of the words "creepy and frightening" that sounded like a brand of delicious cereal. She'd jump every single time the Crypt Keeper came out of his coffin and it made me laugh hard. This would usually wake Nagymama, who'd discover my untucked bed and start screaming "The child is missing!" After barreling into Anyu's room and discovering my location, she'd call Anyu an unfit parent and scramble around in the kitchen drawers for the fakanál to whip us both. Anyu would run into the kitchen to defend us. I would shut the door slowly and unsympathetically so I could hear the TV better.

By the time they were done arguing I'd be asleep in Anyu's bed. In the morning I'd wake up in my own bed, comfortably swaddled. When I woke up, I had to call for Anyu or Nagymama to come retrieve me. Then I'd ask them for the extension cord so I could watch more TV. This type of ritual went on until I was a teenager.

CHAPTER 4: THE SURPRISE

IT WAS A PERFECTLY beautiful and sunny day, but I was five years old and content indoors, watching television while drawing mermaids and avoiding Nagymama's requests for me to come outside. As soon as I had learned how to walk without falling on my face, Nagymama recruited me to walk buckets of water back and forth between the side of the house and her vegetable garden, which was in the back of the property. I asked if we could purchase a hose or sprinkler like people had on TV, but Nagymama assured me that hoses were exorbitantly expensive and a "vaste of vater." I'm pretty sure I spilled more water on myself in a day hauling buckets back and forth than a hose could drip in a lifetime, but as a five year old, my debate skills were not great. Anyu, my court-appointed defender, tried the argument that I should not go outside because there were snakes I might step on and the sun would give me the aforementioned freckles that would make me undesirable to future mates. She would then go through a list of mates she thought were appropriate for me. "Someday," she'd mutter, "Vhen you become a voman."

On one particular day of bucket avoidance, I happened to glance out the window and see Soni, the church lady, talking to Anyu in the driveway. We knew Soni and her daughter, Lisa, from my cousins' Pioneer Girls group, which is like Girl Scouts but sells religion instead of cookies.

Lisa sat in the passenger's seat of the car applying lip balm. Soni was pulling black garbage bags out of her trunk as Anyu shifted uncomfortably. I squeezed behind the television stand and moved the cans of cat food and pot lids Nagymama kept on the windowsill to deter intruders. I wasn't strong enough to open the windows, locked shut even in the middle of the summer (to deter both robbers and kidney colds), so I pressed my ear against the window to hear her. Soni said that Lisa had outgrown her clothes and toys. They wanted to make a charitable donation to my family because they'd heard that my mother lost her job. As much as I wanted to go outside to see what toys I was getting, I was worried I'd get into trouble or nabbed by the Nagymama Gardening Police. Anyu agreed to accept the donations and dragged a few garbage bags onto the steps. She faked a smile as Soni and Lisa pulled away in their giant green gas guzzler and then ran inside to make a frantic phone call.

I tried to sneak out the front door to take a peek at the bags, but Nagymama nabbed me.

"Oh, good, you outside. I swear, you gonna burn your eyes out vith that television."

Before I knew it, I was carrying buckets of water back and forth while craning my neck to watch my mother drag garbage bags into her spicy mustard-colored 1979 Dodge Aspen station wagon. As she lifted one of the bags into the trunk, I saw a shocking piece of triangular pink plastic poke through the bag.

A dollhouse!

As quickly as it had appeared, it disappeared again, into the depths of the monstrous car. Before I could protest, my mother walked through the door and announced that we'd be going to Neni's lake house for the weekend. I stopped in my tracks.

Now everything made sense; the dollhouse was a surprise! I figured Lisa was the little girl the mailman had accidentally delivered my dollhouse to and I was finally going to get it. I deduced that I wasn't supposed to see the dollhouse because they were going to bring it to the lake house and let me set it up there so Barbie could have lakefront property. Neni and Nagymama were always talking about how lakes increased something called property value, so this made total sense. I pretended that I didn't see any of the bags because I was afraid they'd take them away from me for ruining the surprise.

For almost a week, I waited to get my dollhouse. The day came and my family loaded into mom's old Dodge. I sat on the hump between my cousins, who, as typical disinterested Westernized teens, were not nearly as excited as I was to be going on a trip. Probably because they were not about to get an awesome dollhouse, I thought.

As close as I ever got to visiting botanical gardens.

My cousins referred to the lake house in northern New Jersey as the Slanty Shanty, which it technically was. My aunt and uncle had purchased it years ago at a severely discounted rate with the understanding that part of the house was sinking and needed to be repaired immediately. They never fixed it. There was one part of the house that was no longer safe to stand in; they kept inflatable rafts there. The entire house smelled like mold. There were bug carcasses everywhere. Everything that was supposed to have water in it did not and everything that wasn't supposed to have water in it was wet. The lake itself looked like an oil spill, less of an ecosystem and more of a prison for the world's brownest and least interesting fish.

My uncle owned a bunch of pieces of property, a successful liquor store, and an upholstery shop, so my cousins were accustomed to much nicer accommodations. I didn't notice the lake house's problems because its imperfections mimicked those of my own house, right down to the shade of Yak Puke Green paint. But I liked going to the lake house.

Mostly because of the cute homemade ice cream shop at the side of the road we always stopped at on the way there and back.

On this particular occasion, Nagymama did not come with us to the lake house. With no family figurehead to keep us in line, as soon as we stopped at the ice cream shop, the women exploded out of the car in a cacophony of bilingual screaming and complaining. Each of us disappeared into a separate part of the shop. My mother immediately went to the ladies' room, where I knew she'd empty the plastic Halloween pail—a McDonald's Happy Meal bucket shaped like a jack-o'-lantern—which she carried around with her to urinate in because she was afraid of public restrooms.

My cousins ran to the back corner, as far from us as possible, to gossip in horror about how yes, Anyu had peed in the car while we were driving because this was more hygienic than sitting on a public toilet. They'd stop shrieking occasionally to look out the window at a cute teenage boy who was helping his father carry a large leaky cooler to an adjacent picnic area.

This left me alone with the ice cream board, taunting me with its forbidden flavors. Anyu and Nagymama never allowed me to eat any desserts that had colors in them for fear I'd stain my clothing. Because we didn't own a washing machine, I would have to wear the same outfit for about a week until Nagymama washed it in the bathtub and hung it out to dry in the yard. Sometimes they could get more than a week out of my clothes if Anyu was fastidious about putting bibs on me, specifically bibs she stole from McDonald's. Artificial food colorings often would not rinse out if they dripped past the bib; thus, they were forbidden. I basically had to eat my meals wearing a plastic bag with The Hamburglar on it until I was a teen, when I had the dexterity to remove bibs and was physically stronger than my mother. Luckily, Neni owned a washing machine, and she didn't have such phobias.

"Get vhat you vant," Neni said.

"A black raspberry ice cream on a sugar cone. With chocolate sprinkles."

When Neni handed it to me, I tried to gobble it down before Anyu and the jack-o'-lantern exited the bathroom. Sugar cones were also forbidden because Anyu thought they'd break my teeth, and she felt that sprinkles were tiny razor blades that would rip my esophagus open. I thought for sure Anyu would bust me, but she didn't seem to notice the forbidden treat and was more preoccupied with pacing around.

"I touched the garbage bags. Do you think it's safe for me to eat? I vashed my hands a couple times to be sure but. . ."

"Sit down, please," Neni said. "There's ice cream for you." She pointed to a cup of vanilla soft serve that she had purchased for Anyu.

Anyu relaxed. I was relieved there was no explosion. As a child, the relief came with not getting in trouble for ice cream. As an adult looking back, the relief comes with the appreciation of Neni, the only person in Anyu's life who's able to stop her panic episodes and bring her into the moment.

For the first time that whole trip there was silence, save for the munching sounds of everybody eating their ice cream cones. To a casual observer, we looked like a normal American family.

When we got back in the car for the last leg of the ride to the lake, I peered back every so often to make sure that the dollhouse bag was still there, careful to look only when Anyu was screaming at traffic, pedestrians, pot holes, and other miscellaneous things that could not hear her because she always insisted on driving with the windows closed.

After another hour of being jabbed in the ribs with pointy teenager elbows, we arrived at the lake house, which was an eyesore compared to the fifteen other well-kept colonial homes nestled on our side of Cranberry Lake. Irina sighed deeply as we parked in the farthest lot away from the house. "Why do we always need to park a billion miles away? Man, this is so lame."

"Shh! The neighbor vill hear you," Neni said.

Parking was frequently an issue because Joe, one of the lake house neighbors, hogged the spots with his broken down classic cars. Although my family has been known to be outspoken, my mother and aunt were raised to never make waves with men who were the same age or older than they were. "You never know who is good marriage material," Anyu always said. Of course, Anyu and Neni were so non-confrontational that not only did they not say anything to Joe but they also tried to run whenever he was out watering his plants in order to avoid him completely. To this day, Joe probably has no idea how much mental energy was exerted due to his sheer existence. I'd bet his rusty 1960s Pontiac GTO is still sitting in my aunt's assigned parking spot.

After some shushing and bickering, my family dragged their luggage and many garbage bags through the overgrown jungle that was our unkempt side yard.

"Why didn't you guys bring a lawnmower?" Erin asked.

"Yah, yah, I meant to but forgot," Neni said.

"Yeah, like you and Dad meant to fix the planks on the boat garage until they rotted through and the speedboat floated away?" Irina said.

Neni jumped in. "Oh, that reminds me. Did you hear about the lake neighbor, Ramon?" No one knew or cared who Ramon was. It didn't matter. "He vas painting the bottom of his speedboat and the brace gave out? His vife came home and saw his head got crushed by the boat! And then she vent insane."

"You shouldn't tell morbid stories in front of a little kid!" Erin yelled.

"Vhat? How else vill she know not to paint the bottom of boats?" Neni argued.

We managed to pull the bags through the tangle of weeds, but one of the bags ripped, spreading shoes and itchy sweaters everywhere. There was general chaos until Neni ran up to get another garbage bag. She wore a pair of stained gardening gloves to prevent getting poked by the thistles now embedded in our clothing. I reached out to grab a stuffed animal with my bare hands, which caused Anyu to launch into an absolute frenzy. Anyu methodically dragged me by the elbow up the rickety staircase and sat me down on the old plaid couch, instructing me not to move an inch.

I couldn't do anything but look at the taxidermied fish mounted above the foyer, its face preserved in a permanent state of screaming, as my family retrieved the rest of our belongings from the car. I spotted the infamous triangular bag in the corner of the room. The excessive pulling, pushing, and dragging had left several quarter-sized holes in the bag, and I could clearly see the pink plastic siding and the purple shutters. As I reached for it, Anyu walked through the door.

"Vhat did I say?" she said. "No touching! Now, go pee so ve can go get firevood and things from the store!"

I had several issues with this request. First and foremost, I wanted to play with the dollhouse and did not want to go to the firewood store. Second, rather than driving to get firewood, my family enjoyed crossing the entire lake using the longest, most rickety swinging wooden bridge on the planet, and then carrying heavy firewood back across the same bridge by hand. This is an example of what Neni would consider a shortcut.

The third issue was that peeing at the lake house was an unpleasant, multistep process. It required going into the horribly scary bathroom with no light, trying to find the toilet, and then promptly going down to the lake with a bucket, washing your hands with the weird-smelling lye soap, and bringing the bucket full of soapy water back upstairs in order to flush the waterless toilet. I'd never done this myself at the lake house, mind you. I'd just watched Anyu do it because she peed with the door open. At this point I had still never used a big toilet before, instead relying on my trusty potty, and I wasn't about to start today.

"Come on, go to the bathroom already. It's getting dark out!" Irina scolded.

"Vait, vait, vait!" Anyu yelled. Out of one of the garbage bags, she pulled out a little plastic potty and potty bucket and placed it down in the middle of the living room.

"Hooray!" I said, immediately pulling my pants down in front of my entire family.

Erin and Irina screamed in disgust.

"What is it with your side of the family and crapping in public?" Erin said. "Why isn't she potty trained?"

"What is she, six?" Irina asked.

"Five, but I'm a big girl!" I said, midstream.

"Vhat's the problem? She's potty trained. See? Plastic potty. No germs."

"Stephie starts school in September. You need to teach her how shit on the toilet," said Neni.

"She's fine," Anyu said. "They teach her how to shit in kindergarten."

I not only had no idea what being potty trained meant, I also had no idea what school was. Nobody had ever mentioned it to me, and for the most part, the entire conversation went over my head.

It was dark by the time we arrived at the bridge. Anyu and Neni were too engrossed discussing the weight fluctuations of every woman who went to our church to notice my terrified yelps as my cousins swung the bridge to and fro, laughing maniacally.

"Oh no, it's gonna fall," Erin laughed.

"Good thing we both know how to swim. Oh, wait, Stephanie doesn't know. Guess she's gonna drown!" Irina said.

I yelped and cried for what might have been twenty seconds or four hours. In my memory, it is a haze of fear. But eventually we arrived at the wood store.

Anyu and Neni bought some lighter fluid and kindling for the fireplace. The store was on the main road, so it seemed like we were only off the bridge for seconds before we had to go back onto it. I was terrified my cousins were going to tease me again on the way back. I stood at the entrance, hysterically bawling, and wrapped my arms around a nearby telephone pole, refusing to cross the bridge. The reason for this eluded everybody. Anyu and Neni hadn't noticed the initial teasing. My cousins had forgotten about the trip across, never mind recall (or notice) its long-term traumatic effect on me, and were discussing bras and 1987 pop culture references. With no other context to explain the crying, my aunt pried me off the pole and carried my weeping body across the bridge, lamenting what a spoiled and rotten child I was.

With nothing else to do back at the lake house, my cousins immediately opened a mildew-filled Candyland. As an only child, playing a board game with two other kids was a treat. For a moment, I forgot about the dollhouse in the other room and the bridge trauma. I fell into the world of Plumpy and Queen Frostine in the Gumdrop Mountains. I heard Neni gathering the wood for a fire; Anyu pulled out radish-and-margarine sandwiches for us from the cooler. We munched on our dinner while Neni lit the fire. For a moment, the lake house felt cozy.

Then Anyu put on a pair of plastic gloves, grabbed one of the garbage bags, and asked Neni something inaudible.

This is it, I thought. I'm gonna get my dollhouse!

Anyu rooted through the garbage bags and pulled out the Barbie Glamour House. Sure, some of the pieces were a little loose, but they were all there. I could see a canopied swing for two. A rooftop garden patio for grilling. A spiral staircase led up to a beautiful bedroom with a garden view. The bedroom had a secret wall that changed it into a stylish bath.

Neni picked up the house to inspect it. She considered it for a moment, gazing at the painted curtains and canopies. Then she cracked it over her knee and threw it into the fireplace.

I screamed. I cried.

Neni and Anyu were genuinely confused. They had no idea I was watching them.

"These are Lisa's things. They are not for you," Anyu said, throwing in an unstained shirt with a mermaid on it that looked like it would fit me.

"This is for your protection, Stephie," Neni said, tossing in a Barbie doll that had every original limb.

"You don't vant to catch the asthma, do you?" Anyu said, tossing my remaining hopes and dreams into the fire.

They could not understand my outburst. And I had no idea that this was their own unconventional way of expressing their love. Until that moment, I was not aware that the entire weekend had been planned around traveling to the only fireplace they had access to in order to destroy a pathogen. They explained that they'd had no choice but to take the donation.

"You can't look horses in the faces," Anyu said.

I didn't understand what this had to do with anything. Was a horse somehow responsible for all of this?

"In Soviet Europe, you know what we had for toy? Stick."

But I was a child of the '80s, so vehemently marketed to by major corporations that materialism defined nearly all of my childhood aspirations. I believed that commercials were real, and every other child in America had Glamour Houses and extreme toy collections. Anyu and Neni blindly believed Nagymama whenever she diagnosed people with fake infectious diseases, and they also believed every tabloid, 20/20 news report, and horoscope that crossed their paths.

We were all victims of sensationalized media in our own ways, struggling to find safety, happiness, and prosperity amongst the pink plastic falsehoods, headlines of horror, and old wives' tales. But the five-year-old me thought they were mean.

CHAPTER 5: ANAL RETENTIVE

IT HURT when I peed. Not in the "drink some cranberry juice and get some Monistat" kinda way. My bottom was so big that I no longer fit on the plastic toddler potty. I had to jam myself in it and hold up my own weight so I didn't tip it over and spill assorted fluids all over myself. This was not by choice. Despite suggestions from Neni, Erin, and Irina to get me big potty trained, Anyu remained ambivalent on the subject, more trusting of the jack-o'-lantern bucket than any germ-filled, Western-style commode. She also did not feel like arguing with Nagymama, who was convinced I'd fall into the bowl and drown. She saw it on a TV program once. To protect me, Nagymama explained that there was a man hiding inside of the toilet, a man who would grab my butt and suck me down into the sewer forever. I learned much later in life that this sort of thing only happens on crowded subways.

Ironically, the little potty was directly across from the object of my fear—the big potty. I was getting so big that I was face-to-face with the big beast of bottom burden on a day-to-day basis. I found myself asking life's important questions: Who is the man in the toilet? How did he get there? Did he haunt every toilet or just ours? Did he have to check his own toilet to make sure there was no poo-ier man getting ready to suck his butt down even farther? The mystery plagued me. It plagues me still.

The bathroom was dangerous. From the moment I learned of the existence of this toilet person, whenever I went to the bathroom to brush my teeth, use the little potty, or take a bath, I'd close the lid of the big potty with Nagymama's back scratcher and cover the lid with miscellaneous shampoo bottles. If I couldn't reach the shampoo bottles, I'd pile some of my McDonald's Happy Meal toys on top of the lid to weigh it down so the man couldn't get me.

The thought of The Man in the Toilet haunted me at all times.

One day when I tried to sit down on the plastic potty, I found my butt wouldn't fit anymore, no matter how I squeezed. A wave of terror washed over me.

I walked over to the big potty and lifted the lid with great trepidation. I glanced into the bowl and was surprised to see that there was no man inside. I figured he was hiding, though, waiting for my butt to make an appearance. I looked up and spotted a shiny metal handle on top of the toilet. Curious, I pulled on it. To my horror, it made a loud *bawoosh* sound, and the bowl started to fill with water.

I ran out of the bathroom, screaming.

From her bedroom, my mother sighed. "Stephie, quit playing with the toilet. You're vasting vater."

I couldn't trust her with this new information. Our relationship had not been the same since the dollhouse incident. I didn't trust Nagymama either, since she had given my Dream Glow Barbie away to a child at church that I presumed she liked better than me. Everyone was against me – Anyu, Nagymama, the Poo Man. I secretly decided that I'd never go potty again. So I held it. And held it. Until the next day, when Nagymama presented an empty poo bucket to us at the dinner table.

"There's nothing in the pail today," Nagymama said.

Anyu sighed. "She's probably constipated from eating only hot dogs last week."

Nagymama stood with her hands on her hips. "Hot dogs don't make you constipated; it's the shitty Mac-Donald food you always feed to her! I made good soup. She needs to eat more blood!"

She pointed to the fresh batch of awful in the cauldron on the back of the stove. Under the inch of chicken fat, lay a festering lagoon of urine-colored liquid with smidgeons of peppercorns and parsley. There pooled sporadic carrots, overcooked spaghetti shreds, and my favorite, chicken bones and marrows of all shapes and sizes, some disguised as celery, each ready to gouge and shred its way down my throat. Buried imperceptibly within the overall horror were precisely two grains of Morton's iodized salt and three grains of paprika from a 30-year-old spice jar. For flavor. Each week Nagymama made a vat of this slop and left it bubbling and smelling on the stove for days. It was basically a fourth really quiet family member.

"Whatever, it doesn't matter, I'll get the kúp," said Anyu.

A kúp is a glycerin enema, mainly put into children's rectums. It is primarily used to provoke a laxative effect and to cause major psychological scars.

I protested. I was getting better at hiding and squirming, so after enough shenanigans, my mother called the neighbors over for assistance so she could finish her hot dog paprikas in peace.

"Hallo, Dimitri? Remember how you unclogged the gutters by jamming a pole or something up there? My daughter, she is also clogged. In the butt. Got any ideas?"

After a few minutes, Dimitri and his wife, Olga, arrived on our doorstep. Anyu instructed Dimitri to grab one of my arms. She would grab the other, Nagymama would hold my legs, and Olga could do the honors.

As the *kúp* inched towards my bottom, I screamed, "I never want to poop again! The man will get me!"

Dimitri looked concerned. "Vhat man?" he asked.

Olga's eyebrows shot up. "Is there a bad man bothering you *down there*?"

I sniffed. "Nagymama says if I poop, a man in the toilet will come and suck my butt down forever!"

Olga shook her head. "There is no man in the toilet."

"Yes there is! Nagymama said so!"

Nagymama muttered something under her breath.

Olga put the kúp down. "I know what to do."

The adults left the room and whispered angrily in the kitchen. I pulled up my pants and sat in the corner to play with my makeshift dollhouse. I knew for sure that the toilet in the cardboard condominium I designed had no creepy toilet men inside of it because I didn't draw any. And the Barbie Toilet Man™ accessory is sold separately.

The adults returned to the room and Olga sat down next to me. "Now, listen, Stephie," she said in her calmest voice. "I vant you to sit on the big potty and poop like a good girl. Ve'll be there to protect you."

"No, I don't wanna."

"Do it for us once. Jesus vill be there to protect you, too." She pointed at the rosary around her neck.

We walked to the bathroom holding hands, and I hesitantly sat on the big potty. My legs dangled over the edge. The rest of the group watched from the hallway. Olga showed me her rosary and told me to repeat after her, "Dear Jesus, Lord and Savior…"

I shut my eyes and concentrated. "Dear, dear Jesus Lord and Saber—"

"Savior," she corrected me. "*Save*-your."

I opened my eyes. "Save your butt from bad men in the toilet?"

"Yes, Jesus will save your butt from all evil. A-men."

"All-men."

Plop. It worked! Dimitri and Olga were proud of me. Nagymama uncomfortably puttered nearby, refusing to admit any wrongdoing. Anyu was listening from the kitchen, finishing her now-cold paprikas.

"See, Stephie?" Dimitri said. "If you pray to Jesus, he vill protect you from the man in the toilet."

"And the Boogie Man under your bed," Anyu said sarcastically from the kitchen.

I did not yet understand sarcasm. "Boogie Man?" My eyes went wide in terror.

Olga and Dimitri looked at each other and sighed, realizing that this was going to be a long night.

CHAPTER 6: THE OTHER-OTHER PARENT

AUGUST, 1987. It was only noon and already 87 degrees outside. I was the only person in the Bennigan's parking lot who wasn't interested in the wholesome family restaurant and its dual rarities of air conditioning and wacky indoor traffic lights.

I was upset because my father was there. Anyu assured me that I'd met this man three years earlier, when I was two, but apparently my memory was wiped clean. The man I knew as my father lived in the television. This was a stranger who had come to take me away. The only way to prevent this was to weep and avoid eye contact.

My father was accompanied by his new wife, Gabby, who Anyu referred to as "Vife Numbah Tree," and my two teenage half-sisters, Janice and Katie, from his first marriage.

"Come on, everyone," Gabby said. "Hug! You're sisters!"

This upset me more. I had just seen *Invasion of the Body Snatchers* on TV, and in my child-version of the scenario, I assumed that these two teenagers had come to replace the other teens in my life, Irina and Erin. Although Irina and Erin were only cousins, I spent a lot of time with them and looked up to them as big sisters. These other sisters were strangers. And aliens, probably.

I wrapped my arms around Anyu's legs. She attempted to robot walk into the restaurant's foyer with me still attached to her because this was easier than calming me down. "Stephie, if you're a good girl, ve'll buy you a Barbie backpack after ve're done with food," she said.

"You didn't buy her no backpack yet? She starts school soon," my father scolded.

"How am I supposed to buy anything with no child support money? I lost my job!" Anyu said.

"Let's not start a meal off with a fight," Gabby pleaded.

I had no idea what a backpack was, but the mention of a Barbie-related something managed to instantly buy my love. I let go of Anyu's legs and calmed down. I guess my whole family could have gone to hell as long as I got a Barbie in the end.

I relaxed even more when I saw the familiar faces of Erin, Irina, and Neni, who'd arrived at the restaurant early to reserve a table for what to us was an unusually large party. The table was long and rectangular, assembled with four chairs on each side and one seat at the head of the table.

Each family member claimed a seat at the table, unintentionally sitting across from their Bizarro World doppelganger. Erin vs. Janice: Who had the crimpiest, blondest hair and best New Kids on the Block shirt? Irina vs. Katie: Who could mumble the best sarcastic joke to themselves, thus negating its efficacy? Neni vs. Gabby: Who could keep their side of the family from escalating conflict into a mashed potato fight? And Anyu vs. me: Who was more uncomfortable with the vampire guy sitting at the head of the table?

My father held court and ordered lunch for everyone since he spoke better English than my side of the family. Everyone was fine with this until he got to me.

"The child and I will have the spaghetti and meatballs lunch special."

"Stephie can't have that," Anyu said. "She's going to get the red sauce on herself."

"You're micromanaging what she eats but she doesn't know how to speak English or write any words in Hungarian?"

"It's better if she doesn't understand everything that's going on," Anyu said.

Neni pondered for a moment. "How's Stephie gonna talk to the teacher if she don't talk good?"

"Maybe she has a learning disability?" Gabby asked.

"No vay," my father said. "She's smart 'cuz she got the best genes from me."

Despite the importance of the adult conversation that was happening around me, I was distracted by the presence of the teenagers. Not only did they speak English, but they also had their own '80s slang that went over my head. They laughed and compared their bangle bracelets, Casio watches, and movie star crushes. I showed them the new outfit I'd made Barbie, consisting of a marker-and-masking-tape dress, but they were not interested.

The waiter came by with a giant plate of what I thought was silly string covered in paint surrounded by rubber balls. He placed it in front of my father. I tried to reach for it but my arms were too short. The waiter continued to serve the table.

"Why hasn't she learned to speak English from other kids on the playground?" Gabby asked.

"I don't take her to the playground. I don't vant her to go blind from the cat pee," my mother replied.

Everyone nodded gravely except for Gabby, who hadn't heard of the family superstition.

"I don't understand," she said. "What cat?"

Neni's smile grew into an evil smirk befitting The Grinch. One of her favorite hobbies was telling long-winded, alarmist, and graphic stories about old-world superstitions. This particular wives' tale involved an overseas family member who went blind because cat fecal bacteria ate through her young innocent eyeballs as a result of playing one time on a playground in a neighborhood where a cat lived. The true story, I learned much later, is that the girl had retinitis pigmentosa, a genetically inherited disease. To this day, this does not stop my aunt from publicly shaming the poor woman's mother at every opportunity for allowing her daughter to play in a sandbox.

Neni stabbed a meatball violently with a fork to demonstrate worms burrowing into a cornea.

"Wait," Gabby said. "If Stephanie has never been to a playground, does she know how to play on a slide or swingset?"

Everyone shook their head no.

"Then she's going to hurt herself when the school lets her out for recess!" Gabby said.

"Oh, no, Stephie, she needs to stay inside," Anyu said. "I no fill out the permission slip for her to go outside."

My father rolled his eyes. "There's no permission slip for recess, you vacko."

Gabby kicked him under the table. "Lajos, have some respect for the mother of your child."

The waiter brought me a plate like my father's, covered with red silly putty. I put my whole arm into it. It was warm and pleasantly squishy.

"No! The red sauce. It vill stain!" Anyu cried.

"I got it," Gabby continued, ignoring my mother and me. "We're buying her a swing set. Tonight."

"Listen, voman. I'm not made of money," my father said.

"Hush, now. You've never been a part of this child's life. It's time to make up for it so she doesn't cry every time she sees you. Teach her how to use a swing set."

Curious, I took a meatball and banged it against the table, assuming it would bounce like a rubber ball. Instead, it rolled, leaving a greasy orange slime trail and plopping into Irina's lap. She jumped up to reveal a huge stain on her acid-wash shorts.

"You're such a barf bag, Stephanie," Irina said. She threw down her napkin and ran to the bathroom.

"You see? The stain! Eat it, don't throw," Anyu scolded and shoved a fork full of spaghetti into my mouth.

I chewed tentatively. Even as a child, I was a night person, so I was never hungry during breakfast or lunch. My family liked going to lunch because it was cheaper, but the smell of food at the beginning of the day turned my stomach. I preferred to play with it.

"Gag me with a spoon. I am never having kids," Janice said.

"Yeah, lame. Like, isn't she a little old to be flinging food?" Katie asked.

"Look! You're eating worms," Erin said, knowing I'd never eaten spaghetti before.

I looked down. Indeed, in my child's mind, there were wriggling worms on my plate. I spit the spaghetti everywhere.

"Psych!" Erin said.

"This rotten child doesn't need a swing set. She needs a swing of the fakanál," Neni said.

"Excuse me, what did you call her?" Gabby asked, assuming that Neni had dropped an f-bomb at the lunch table.

"No, no, not a bad word, just a spoon we beat the kids with," said Neni.

Gabby raised her eyebrows at my father.

Undeterred, my father finished his entire plate and mine. After leaving the restaurant and driving to the mall, I decided that I was hungry. The rest of the family stayed at the mall, while Anyu and I went back to our house.

As I sat patiently while Anyu made me a sandwich, she vented, half to herself, half to me.

"Gabby, so fat, she looks fat, don't you think she's fat?"

"Can I have green peppers *and* radishes on my sandwich?"

"Yah, okay. He said he vanted you aborted, you know. I have the letter. He said he vould turn you against me someday if I had you. So don't trust him, you know. Margarine or butter?"

"Um. Margie ram."

"Okay."

The family reconvened at the house. Gabby proudly presented me a Barbie lunchbox and backpack. I accepted graciously and attempted to figure out what these odd new accessories were for. My father spent the last few hours before sunset pouring concrete, slamming around metal swing pieces, and cussing. He could no longer bear women hovering around him. With one mighty man roar, he banished the eight of us to the tiny living room.

Because there was only room for two people on the pull-out couch that doubled as Nagymama's bed, I joined the teens sitting cross-legged on the floor. Erin flicked through the channels and found nothing but snow. She didn't know the trick: holding the antenna above your head for the duration of the show you wanted to watch. I poured a cup of water into the Barbie Lunchbox, assuming it was a Barbie Oddly Rectangular Swimming Pool, splashing Irina.

"Haven't you destroyed enough of my clothing today?" she asked.

I giggled. I thought I was one of them now.

"Yuck, you don't have cable? How are we supposed to watch *DeGrassi*?" Janice asked.

"*DuckTales! DuckTales!*" I suggested, carefully stuffing Barbie after Barbie into the backpack, which I assumed was a big communal Barbie bed.

"You're sitting too close to the TV," Neni said.

Anyu nodded. "Shut it off or you'll burn your eyes out."

Nagymama dragged chairs from the kitchen into the living room. "Get off the floor! Kidney colds!"

"My kidneys are very warm inside of my body," Irina said into her shirt so she was audible only to her sister and me.

Erin rolled her eyes. "These things do not exist. I'm going to buy you all a Hungarian medical book."

"Do you think they have kidney colds in Hungarian medical books?" asked Janice.

"It's probably the only thing in the book," said Katie, popping some Bubblicious gum. She imitated Nagymama's accent, "Kidney colds are dah root of all dah diseases!"

The teens laughed. Ignoring them, Nagymama shuffled papers she retrieved from inside of the piano bench.

"Nagymama has a surprise for you," said Anyu.

For the four hours that it took for the concrete outside to set, Nagymama played folk songs, intermingled with an orchestral variation of "Life Goes On" by the Beatles, on an out-of-tune piano. After she ran through her repertoire of five songs, she replayed the same songs. Everyone clapped politely, looking around for implements that could be used to destroy the piano and make the destruction look like an accident. In those few hours, I learned from the older girls how to turn dozens of Howard Johnson's placemats into paper airplanes, paper boats, paper fortune tellers, and paper cranes.

It was nearly sundown before we were able to use the swing set. Anyu forbade me from using the slide because it was too steep and the monkey bars because they were too high. I was only allowed to use the swing, which Anyu hung exactly four inches from the ground. While I attempted swinging, which was essentially rubbing the backside of my legs in the dirt, I watched the teens play on the slide and monkey bars with great ease.

To celebrate, Gabby poured the adults glasses of Pálinka, a traditional Hungarian fruit brandy. "Look at how happy everyone is. Everything is going to change now," she said. "We'll come visit more. We're going to be a family."

While everyone was distracted, I climbed up onto the ladder, reached as far as I could, and let myself dangle on the first monkey bar. Even with a summer's worth of lugging water jugs back and forth to the garden, I lacked the coordination and upper body strength to get to the next bar. I landed right on my ankle. It hurt, but I knew I'd be in trouble if I cried out so I sucked in my breath and thought about mermaids.

There was no fooling Anyu, though. She had mommy radar. She turned around as soon as she heard the thump. She ran over to me and saw that my ankle was twisted.

The joy of childhood.

Less than an hour later, my sprained ankle was the size of a baseball.

Less than a month later, my father was out of the country. His marriage to Vife Numbah Tree was over. He said he was bored with the marriage. She said he stole her identity and put her into over $200,000 worth of debt. I'll never know the truth.

My father told me in a postcard that I no longer had a stepmother. And I should stop calling her. He also mentioned that I no longer had a subscription to *National Geographic: Kids* because National Geographic had gone out of business (not because it was his ex-wife who had been paying the twelve dollar annual subscription fee). He mentioned he'd be back soon. I didn't lay my eyes on him for another twenty years.

The year that my father was in a relationship with Gabby was the only time my mother ever regularly received child support payments. This was good because we did not have health insurance, and I needed an air cast and rehabilitation therapy for my ankle. The doctor said I would have to stay in bed for six weeks.

I still didn't have a firm grasp on the concept of kindergarten and the fact that it was looming. I was blissfully ignorant that as a result of my injury I'd be starting school several weeks after the other children. For a few glorious weeks I didn't have to water Nagymama's vegetable garden. Anyu was relieved because I couldn't move and therefore could not hurt myself further. She even gave me a little bell, like a princess. Whenever I rang it, radish sandwiches appeared. I spent my days drawing, looking at magazines filled with animals, watching cartoons, and examining my mysterious new Barbie accessories. I didn't have a care in the world.

CHAPTER 7: KINDERGARTEN

AT FIRST, I thought that having a sprained ankle was the best thing that could have ever happened to me. But even television addicts can get cabin fever. The cast was itchy and I was bored. After I noticed leaves outside my window turning a pretty orangey-red color, I began to obsess over how much I wanted to crunch them under my feet. Anyu forbade me from using crutches because she thought I'd fall and break my face open on the concrete. But when she went out for her daily errands, Nagymama would carry me outside and prop my leg up on a picnic table for an hour or two, telling me this would stop me from looking pale and horrid.

On the third or fourth day that Nagymama snuck me outside, Natasha, the next-door neighbor's three-legged German Shepherd, saw me and jumped over the back gate. Her collar made a jingling sound as she trotted over to me. She sniffed at an empty Happy Meal box on the ground near my uninjured foot. I felt nervous but curious. I'd never pet a dog before. She licked my French-fry-salt-encrusted hand and I giggled. Her nose was cold.

When Anyu got home, Nagymama went over to unlock the Kapu so Anyu could pull the station wagon into the driveway. She'd forgotten that I was outside. Anyu and Nagymama immediately got into an argument over something.

I called to get their attention. "Anyu, look a doggie!"

She glanced over. She locked eyes with me. She locked eyes with Natasha. She pushed past Nagymama and started running across the lawn. "No, Stephie, it's gonna eat off your face!"

The dog was sniffing its own butt. Upon seeing Anyu run towards her, she gently hopped back over the back gate and ran to chew lightly on some dandelions next to her doghouse.

Dress to impress with Kmart's new line of sweatpants, sweatshirts, and clown shoes.

"You never talk to strange dogs again vithout my permission!" Anyu said, taking me inside.

That night she showed me graphic pictures of dog attacks. She'd clipped them out of magazines and laser copied them out of books at the library throughout the years, saving them for just this occasion. She also reminded me of the dangers of cats and their urine. The graphic images burned themselves into my head. I developed an irrational fear of dogs from that point on.

Three weeks later, and a few days after my cast was removed, I went into the kitchen to ask if I could go play outside, but I heard only hushed whispers coming from Anyu's bedroom. I knew something was up because Anyu and Nagymama were speaking Romanian. They emerged to find me standing right outside the door.

Anyu looked at me suspiciously from the corner of her eye and said something to Nagymama in Romanian.

"What's happening? Is it going to hurt?" I asked.

It's not that Romanian is an evil-sounding language. It's a Romance language; most words said in it sound nice. But the last few times they'd used it, I'd gotten a cavity filled, a shot at the doctors, and a dollhouse burned in front of me. I didn't trust it.

"Hush, Stephie, put on your coat," Anyu said. "Nagymama is going to take you for a valk. To the park." Her eyes darted left and right like a cartoon supervillain.

Despite the mild September weather, Nagymama buckled us into matching puffy silver winter coats and shoved an oversized knit pom-pom hat on my head. She donned her usual highly fashionable tricorn hat and handed me my Barbie lunchbox.

"Food inside," she said, refusing to look directly at me. "No let anybody else have it."

My growing fear was erased when I saw the familiar face of Barbie. I couldn't understand why anyone would waste such a wondrous box on food because food already came in its own box, shaped as either a Happy Meal or a Kid's Cuisine.

Crazy Nagymama, I thought.

I squealed with glee as we waddled up the street, hand in hand. Going to the park was an infrequent treat. Our trips to the park awarded me the rare opportunity to play in the sun in the general proximity of other children. Granted, I was never allowed to use the park equipment or speak to the other children. We'd sit on the bench and feed the birds old scraps of bread crust, like two little old people. Sitting on the bench near the Big Slide was forbidden because Nagymama said that's where the bad kids hung out. I didn't know what was bad about them. Perhaps it was because they had bicycles—those were also forbidden.

Mostly, I hung out by the Gray Rock, which used to house a commemorative plaque for the Piscataway Elementary School but now was a blank canvas for graffiti artists to write swear words in Gujarati. I drew princesses on it with waxy crayons.

Today, we walked past the rock, crossed over the sandy patch near the seesaws, stepped beyond the forbidden slide covered in cigarette butts, and pushed open a set of glass double doors leading into a small brick building. On the map within my child brain, this building, and really anything past the park, was the equivalent of "Here, There be Dragons."

"Bemegyünk," Nagymama said, which means, "Go this way unless you want your arm to be pulled out of its socket."

I followed her through the wide doors.

She forcibly pulled me down a long corridor until we turned into an office and were greeted by a gray-haired woman wearing a festive fall sweater.

The lady smiled at us, revealing braces with orange-and-black rubber bands. "Yip yip yip, Stephanie!" she said in an alien language. "Yip yip yip yip?"

"Mi?" I said, which is Hungarian for, "Whatchu talking about, crazy lady?"

Nagymama seemed to understand her. She nodded and pushed me forward. The lady walked us down another hall and opened a door to reveal a room filled with children in brightly colored clothing. It was chaos unlike anything I'd ever seen. To me, they seemed to be screaming and running with scissors, some of them possibly on fire. I grabbed Nagymama's legs and hid behind her. Nagymama gracefully pried me off of her, walked away, and shut the door behind her.

I stared at the closed door for a moment until I began to distinguish foreign voices behind me. The strange lady was waving her arms, indicating that I should sit with a little girl who was gluing macaroni to her shirt. I was torn. The glued-macaroni concept was fascinating, but I wasn't supposed to talk to strangers. Out of the corner of my eye, I saw two other children slapping each other's wrists with magical sticks that would turn into bracelets covered in smiley faces. Everyone was screaming in the same weird language.

Nagymama has left forever, and now I have to live with the Yip-Yip aliens from *Sesame Street*, I thought.

I climbed up to the side window and started banging on it as hard as I could. I cried for Nagymama through the glass, but she couldn't hear me. She didn't even turn around. She puttered out of the parking lot and out of my life, presumably forever. I thought I was dreaming the kind of dream where you scream and scream but nothing comes out. Except for the fact that there was a lot of real screaming coming out, which is why the strange lady had to pick me up by the armpits and place me in a fake kitchen to calm me down. There was a little boy sitting at the kitchen table, grinning at me eerily. I'd never spoken to a little boy by myself before.

"Yip, yip, Stephen," the lady said, exhausted. "Yip yip, Stephanie. Yip?"

"What's up, Doc?" he said to me.

This I understood. The little boy's name was exactly like my name, but in a boy's version. He was also quoting the most famous rabbit I knew. Way more famous than the rabbit Nagymama had skinned and boiled in front of me the previous evening.

The strange lady handed me a plastic plate and a toy baby. It was the kind that automatically blinked its eyes and said "Mama" if you held it at the right angle. Based on what I knew about boys from what I had interpreted from the episodes of *The Young and the Restless* I'd seen on TV, I assumed this meant that Stephen and I were married. I was to prepare Stephen a meal, take care of this child, and plan our escape together. After all, Anyu was always talking about finding me suitors, so I assumed this was somehow her doing. I placed the toy baby in its high chair and looked around the toy kitchen for suitable plastic fruits and vegetables to serve my new husband. I was happy to find a plate of plastic scrambled eggs and bacon, because according to Anyu I wasn't allowed to use the stove. I placed the meal in front of Stephen, and he smiled even wider.

"What's up, Doc?" He threw the food to the side. "What's up, Doc?"

"Neeeeem!" My carefully arranged meal was ruined. I looked over to check on the baby. It was gone.

"Hol van a baba?" I cried, gesturing wildly at the high chair.

Stephen shrugged. "What's up, Doc? Doc? Doc? Doc?"

Looking back on it, perhaps the teacher placed us together because we had similar television-based language issues.

I was terribly worried that I'd lost the baby and the strange lady would punish me. Then I noticed an odd shape through the little window in the miniature forbidden oven. I looked left, looked right, and opened the plastic oven door.

It was our baby.

Stephen must have decided to cook the baby while my back was turned. I was sure this was bad. I took the baby and ran out of the classroom screaming, going up the long corridor, heading toward the Gray Rock, where I planned to hide the cooked baby in case the strange lady, Nagymama, or local authorities decided to investigate.

Unfortunately, the lady with the festive braces, who turned out to be my kindergarten teacher, summoned backup from other yipping adults, who turned out to be most of the Piscataway Elementary School administration. They were far less festive.

A set of hands came down and wrapped around my midriff. Startled, I dropped the baby. It skidded across the hall, its voice box cooing a slowing "Mama, Ma-ma, Maaaamaaa" in a manner fit for only the creepiest of horror movies. I continued to run in midair, kicking the person attached to the hands in the groin with the back of my feet. It was the school principal, Mr. Palooza.

They called home. I was immensely relieved when I looked out the window in the principal's office and saw Nagymama tottering towards me. Principal Palooza tried to explain to her what had happened, but her English was almost as bad as mine. We both knew it wasn't good based on his large hand gestures and excessive sweatiness.

Nagymama shrugged at him. "Yah. Okay. See tomorrow. Bye."

In her brain, nothing had gone wrong. It was Anyu's and Nagymama's job to keep me alive, fed, and reasonably clean and clothed, and they'd fulfilled their end of this agreement. They felt that school was the place I should learn about everything else: speaking English, reading, the difference between toy ovens and actual ovens, the birds and the bees, what other children are, what I am, and so on.

I had many questions for Nagymama on the two-block walk from school to my house. Why did the people in that building speak the secret TV language? Who did those children belong to? Am I married to Stephen now? What was going to happen to our baby? Where do babies come from?

Nagymama sighed as we arrived at the house. She knelt down next to me, pointed in the general direction of the school, and opened her mouth.

This would be it, I figured, the answers to all my questions. The confusing world around me would start making sense.

"Don't run," she said, waving the fakanál. She stood back up. No additional explanation to any of my questions. Everything would remain a mystery, except for the very specific "no running in school, under any circumstances," rule. Perhaps this is why I ended up being so bad at gym class.

Nagymama then sat me down in the kitchen, opened the lunchbox, and handed me my sandwich. The pink of the lunchbox seemed to vibrate against the stained table and musty kitchen walls as I ate.

"Finished? Good." Nagymama grabbed the lunchbox from me.

"I wanted to keep that."

"Lunchbox for school! You get tomorrow."

I looked at the lunchbox. It was a thing of beauty, even if its only purpose was to hold radish sandwiches. I had to have it back, even if it meant that I had to learn to yip like everyone else.

CHAPTER 8: THE SCHOOL PICTURE

I FEARED the chipped, circa 1977, mustard–colored bowl in our kitchen cabinet. It was used primarily for whisking eggs, making dough, and measuring out my haircut. I'm not sure if bowl cutting was common practice in the old country, an American fad they picked up, or the brainchild of Nagymama's friend Dimitri, the man who inflicted haircuts on me every six to eight weeks. Dimitri was not a barber. He was our neighbor, unintentional potty training educator, and friendly handyman. I suppose Nagymama figured that if Dimitri could cut our lawn, he could cut my hair.

It was spring and unseasonably warm. I was dressed for winter and sweating like a pig, so I nagged Nagymama to open a window. She said no. I nagged her for a short-sleeved shirt. She said no. I nagged her for a Vanilla Twin Pop to cool down before dinner. She said no.

I walked over to Anyu and before I could open my mouth, she reached in the freezer and handed me the frozen treat. I ripped off the white waxed paper victoriously, but my bliss was cut short when I spotted the notorious bowl on the kitchen table. For a moment, I hoped that Nagymama was going to make palacsinta, a type of Hungarian dessert similar to French crepes, but my hope dimmed when I saw the rusty, green-handled scissors next to the bowl.

I almost dropped my ice cream. I'd managed to survive my indoctrination into American society. I didn't have a lot of friends in kindergarten, but I spoke English, at least well enough to know that tomorrow was Picture Day and this was important. I didn't want to have a stupid haircut everyone would make fun of. They already made fun of me for so many other things.

I looked for a hiding spot. I had previously tried hiding near the trash can amongst the mouse traps and by standing in the back of my mom's closet with her blue bathrobe draped over me. But they always found me. It was tough to hide in a 425-square-foot house.

This time, I tried the hamper, a funny-smelling, bronze-colored vinyl contraption that was kept in the nook between my mother's bedroom and the kitchen. I was small enough to fit in it as long as I crouched down and wrapped my arms around myself.

Stop! Hamper time! It's Hamper, go Hamper, MC Hamper, yo Hamper!

I knew when Dimitri arrived because I could smell his cheap aftershave, even through Nagymama's dirty laundry. I heard soft chitchat a few feet from where I was hiding. I was sucking the remnants of my ice cream off of my fingers when my mother flipped open the hamper flap.

"Sorry for the mess," Anyu said to Dimitri as she threw rags into the hamper and onto my head. "I haven't had a chance to do the vash."

I yelped as the cold, wet rags hit me in the face.

"Stephie! Vhy are you being a veirdo?" She lifted me out of the hamper with ease. "Say hello to our friend, Dimitri."

I struggled and punched her breasts, but she grinned through the pain.

"You remember Dimitri, right? Of course you do, he's Uncle Dimitri, here to make you look pretty!"

I knew it was useless to struggle; it was three against one. I crossed my arms and pouted as they seated me in our uncomfortable, vinyl-padded kitchen chair, the last of a once matching set that had long ago deteriorated into prickly shards. Its white flowers on a blue background were streaked with pieces of duct tape.

"Ve're gonna do some snip-snip-snippy today, yes?" Dimitri asked. His breath reeked of vodka.

I stared at his gray-speckled five o'clock shadow as he placed the bowl on my head. The bowl felt as if it was crushing my precious, still-malleable vertebrae with its weight.

He hummed some semblance of a polka as he snip-snip-snipped away, his shaky hands occasionally slipping and putting an accidental "v" in my perfect ring of hair.

Anyu and Nagymama provided audio commentary the entire time. "Vhat are you doing? It's crooked. Did you remember to mow the lawn in the back part of the house, too? That side is shorter than the other. Don't cheat me. I'm going to check and make sure you mowed the entire lawn! Make sure you trim her bangs good so her hair doesn't poke her eyes out."

For the finale, Nagymama roughly jammed two pink plastic bow barrettes onto my bangs and pinned the extra hair to the side of my head.

Dimitri handed me an old black pocket mirror. "Lookit, you're beautiful."

It was my worst nightmare: I looked like a boy. Not only was my hair way too short but the cut, loose hair had stuck to the ice cream on my face and given me a wispy beard. My hair was already starting to form a cowlick in the back. The barrettes were clipped to make it look as if I had a receding hairline at age six. I burst into tears.

I made a grab for the scissors. I'm going to give you bad haircuts! I wanted to yell, but I wasn't brave enough. If I couldn't overpower the adults, I resolved to hide the scissors. "No! Don't touch scissors," Anyu yelled. "Your eyes, you'll poke out your eyes!"

"I'm gonna look ugly for the picture!" I cried.

Nagymama and Dimitri were instantly bored by my idle threats and screams. They walked away to gossip in the living room, plates full of stale coffee cake.

Anyu was more sympathetic. "If you stop crying, you can pick out the necklace you vant to vear in the school picture," she said.

"Really?" I sniffed.

She nodded and opened the "drawer" where we kept the necklaces, which was an old donut box from the grocery store. I can still remember the sweet smell of plastic combined with powdered sugar. I resolved to wear all the necklaces.

The next morning I went to school, bejeweled like a mini Mr. T. I donned a navy blue pom-pom ski cap to cover my botched hairdo. I tried to hide in the back of the group, but my teacher nabbed me. By now I knew her name to be Mrs. Scharf, not the Festive Sweater Orange Braces Yip-Yip Lady.

"No hats in class, Stephanie," she frowned.

"But my head is. . .cold."

I could hear a few snickers. All eyes were on me.

"Take that hat off right now. I'm going to count to three."

By the time she got to two, I was already revealing the static-enhanced version of my bad haircut, afraid of what would happen if my teacher got to "three."

The entire class erupted in laughter.

"Aha, we have a new boy in class," said Mohan, a slender boy from Gujarat who'd become my number one tormenter, a role he embraced K-12. He was sporting new, hilarious, oversized eyeglasses, but no one seemed to notice because he always knew how to turn the attention on me.

Kiara, a husky African-American girl wearing a purple dress with the words "I'm the Princess!" embroidered on the front, pointed her finger at me. "What's your name, new boy?"

"I bet it's Stephen!" Mohan roared.

"She can't be Stephen. I'm Stephen," said Stephen, not looking at or talking to any of us directly. The sweet boy never picked on me, probably because he was always behind on the jokes.

Kiara decided to add another victim into the mix. "How come Alia gets to wear a hat if none of us can? I want to wear my Strawberry Shortcake Cap."

Alia, a petite girl with almond eyes and a pretty blue scarf that covered her head and chest, shrunk into herself. I knew her from our biweekly English as a Second Language (ESL) classes. We had silently bonded over our obscure primary languages. The Spanish-trained speech instructors were as puzzled by her Arabic as they were by my Hungarian. I felt guilty that she was being shamed on my account.

"Alia gets to wear a scarf because it's her religion," Mrs. Scharf said.

"Nuh-uh. She wears it because she's bald under there," said Maria, a Spanish-speaking girl from our ESL class. She was the coolest kid in the class because she had pierced ears. I was never sure if Maria was my friend or enemy; she would often walk with Nagymama and me after school because she lived a few blocks from us. During these walks, she was mischievous but friendly. She asked me questions directly and treated my grandmother with respect. In class, she teased me with the other kids.

"Quiet, everyone. Stephanie, please sit." Mrs. Scharf, seeing I was visibly upset, put a reassuring hand on my shoulder. "Well, I like your haircut."

Of course she did, I thought. She had the exact same haircut.

*　　*　　*

Later that day, as we were waiting in line to get our pictures taken, Maria came up behind Alia and me.

"If you have hair, prove it." She reached for Alia's head covering.

Alia held onto her scarf instinctively. Maria and Alia seemed to have a history that dated back to preschool, a program I didn't attend. "I told you, no one is allowed to see my hair except for my family."

"Hey, leave her alone," I said and immediately regretted it.

Maria turned to sneer at me. "Your barrettes look stupid." She pulled them out of my hair, threw them in the garbage, and walked to the back of the line to chat with her usual friends.

I was conflicted. I hated the barrettes and I had no desire to dig through the garbage in front of my classmates. But I was also afraid that Nagymama would get angry if I took a picture without them.

Alia interrupted my anxiety loop. "Hey, I like your necklaces."

**Channeling my inner
Balki Bartokomous.**

"Together, they're the prettiest!" I said, for this is how kindergarteners understand fashion.

Soon it was my turn for the picture. The photographer asked me to please pick my top three necklaces before he could take my photo. I sadly removed approximately thirty-seven necklaces and placed them in a heap next to me.

I wasn't sure how to smile. I opened my mouth to show my teeth, resulting in an insincere grimace. The flash popped and I walked away, fascinated by the spots in front of my eyes. I lingered for a second to see how Alia took her picture. She smiled genuinely and posed gracefully, a natural model at age six.

She noticed that I was waiting for her and ran to catch up with me. "Hey! You like Barbie, right?" she asked.

"Um, yes."

"I like her, too."

I didn't know it, but I'd made my first best friend.

CHAPTER 9: THE SECRET DRAWING

"GET YOUR SMOCKS," Mrs. Price, my first grade teacher, announced.

It was the beginning of first grade, and it was time for art class. For the first time, I had to leave the safe walls of our familiar classroom and venture to the mysterious art room across the school. My fellow classmates and I walked in a carefully regulated single-file line down the hall, passing older children who had a freedom in their steps we had not yet learned as terrified youngsters.

We entered a room with a peculiar smell, a combination of sawdust and wax. Children's drawings were hung on the walls, and they were coupled with yellowed reprints of famous works of art I was seeing for the first time. The room had wide and sturdy wooden tables covered in construction paper and crayons.

A broad-shouldered woman with a dark mullet stood with her back to us. I admired the silver chains she wore around her neck that clanked exactly like Natasha the Dog's collar as she furiously scribbled something on the chalkboard.

"Everyone sit down," she said without looking back at us.

Alia was home sick from school that week with the chicken pox. I had no choice but to sit next to Stephen, who I was avoiding because the rumor of us being sister/brother and simultaneously girlfriend/boyfriend was causing additional teasing.

I struggled to climb onto a stool that was intended for older kids and tried to read some of the pencil graffiti that had been etched into the tabletop.

The art teacher turned around and brushed the chalk dust off her ripped jeans. On the chalkboard she'd drawn a heart that contained an elaborate motorcycle with the words *Ms. Hart* written on the seat. She moseyed over to her desk and straddled her chair.

"My name is Ms. Hart and I teach art. I understand the irony. I've heard jokes about other things my name rhymes with, so don't bother."

The classroom went silent as thirty children simultaneously scanned through their mental databases of words that rhymed with "Hart." Someone snickered to himself.

Ms. Hart put her fingers to her lips as if she were taking a drag from an invisible cigarette. "Draw your name into something like I did, okay?" She sighed, as if exhaling cigarette smoke, then sipped coffee out of a chipped mug splattered with bits of paint and plaster.

Kiara raised her hand. "Um, excuse me, Mrs. —"

"*Mizz*," she corrected. "Hart."

"Do we have to draw it in a bicycle?"

"No. Draw it in something you like. I like motorcycles, so I drew my name in a Harley Davidson."

"I like tricycles too. Can I draw it in a tricycle like yours?" Stephen asked.

"It's a motorcycle!" She pounded her fist on the table. Brown liquid from her cup sprayed on her yellow sleeveless shirt, but she didn't seem to care. "And no. I already drew a motorcycle. Pick something else." She sighed again. "Everybody draw something different, okay? You have until the end of class. Then we're going to show them to everyone and hang them in the halls."

Stephen was already going at it, furiously scribbling Michelangelo from *Teenage Mutant Ninja Turtles* with a half-chewed green crayon, stopping only occasionally to chew on it himself. I pouted and looked down at my blank sheet of paper. Michelangelo was my favorite Ninja Turtle too, but I was afraid that I'd get in trouble for drawing the same character. I was also concerned that his Ninja Turtle drawing would be better than mine.

"Boys can draw better muscles than girls," he explained, "because boys have bigger muscles. That's why girls should draw princesses. They don't need muscles."

I decided that I should draw mermaids and princesses publicly and draw Ninja Turtles secretly since I liked them and the idea of having a secret seemed exciting.

After some deep contemplation, I grabbed a yellow crayon and started my masterpiece. We merrily colored for a few minutes before

Ms. Hart walked by our table. She frowned deeply and grabbed Stephen's drawing.

"What is this?" she asked, pointing to the Herculean reptile.

"It's Michelangelo. He's a party dude—"

"Does everyone see this?" Ms. Hart said, showing the drawing to the class. "This is what we call copyrighted material."

We stared at her blankly. No one knew what she was talking about.

"Copyrighted material is artwork that belongs to someone else!"

"But I made it just now," Stephen said.

"Oh, really, Stephen? What if Marvel Comics came in here today? Would you would tell them that you made up that turtle by yourself and you didn't copy it?"

"Nothing would happen if Marvel Comics walked in here because Marvel doesn't represent the TMNT franchise. And besides, this is fair use," Stephen would have said if he were the 30-something geek he is today instead of the doe-eyed first grader who cried and wet his pants a little.

"Drawing cartoon characters from TV and movies is stealing. You could go to jail."

I looked down in horror at my half-completed Flounder from the movie *The Little Mermaid*. I immediately slipped the paper onto my lap and haphazardly scribbled a purple flower with my name in it onto a new sheet of paper.

After a long rant about U.S. copyright laws to a bunch of terrified, confused children, Ms. Hart crumpled up the Ninja Turtle drawing, threw it on the floor, and pulled out a new sheet of paper for Stephen. "Again. This time, don't steal."

She paused for a moment and looked down at my flower.

"You see, class? Stephanie has drawn her *own* flower from her imagination. She's not stealing; she's being creative. You should come and look at Stephanie's flower."

I sunk into my chair. The flower was a farce. As my classmates walked by, I was convinced that their X-ray eyes could peer through my desk and see my illegal Flounder drawing. Stephen sniffed to himself and drew a picture of a boat. My guilt was overwhelming. Soon, the school bell rang and our first grade teacher came back to collect us. While the other kids started to line up and Ms. Hart hung up our public domain drawings, I spotted the crumpled Ninja Turtle on the floor. I grabbed it and stuffed it into my backpack, where I'd also stashed illicit Flounder. Nagymama was not the only person in my family who knew how to pilfer.

I snuck up behind Stephen in our single-file line back to our classroom. "Pssst. I have something for you." I handed him the mangled drawing of Michelangelo and braced myself for rejection or ridicule.

"How did you get this?" he asked.

I looked around to make sure the coast was clear. "Don't tell!" I opened up my backpack to show him Flounder.

His eyes lit up. "Hey, that's pretty good. You're a good draw-er."

"Thanks. I like yours better. I don't know how to draw muscles that good."

"That's okay. I'll show you," he said, stuffing the Michelangelo into his backpack. "Even though you're a girl."

CHAPTER 10: THE COOTIES

THE SUN WAS SHINING and the Easter hyacinths were in full bloom, wafting their delicious scent through the windows, but I was the seven-year-old trying to hide in the back of the group because it was almost my turn to read the flip chart. I was already self-conscious because Mrs. Pine had put me in the Blue Jay group. Everyone wanted to be a Red Robin so they could sit in the circle closest to the windows and be taught by Miss Brown, the beautiful and soft-spoken teacher's assistant.

The Blue Jays at our circle represented the slower reading group, or as the Red Robins referred to us, "the Bo-Bo reading group." I was the worst reader of the Bo-Bos because of my thick accent and terrible stutter that was exacerbated every time I felt anxious.

"Stephanie, it's your turn. Get up here. What does the chart say?"

"Dah…vitch vas on va-va-vacation vith—"

"No. *The* not *D. W* not *V*," Mrs. Pine corrected. She slapped the ruler against the table with each "W" sound. As a former Catholic school administrator, Mrs. Pine often had to resist using what probably would have been highly satisfying corporal punishment on us. "The witch was on vacation with her friend Veronica."

A series of dings went off, signaling that there was an important announcement coming on the loudspeaker. Mrs. Pine gestured for me to sit down. I was relieved.

"There is a severe head lice epidemic at the school," Principal Palooza announced. "The nurse will call classrooms in one at a time tomorrow to check each and every student."

Kiara turned from her Red Robin circle and gave me an evil smile. Her newly braided hair made tiny plastic clinking noises every time she moved her head. "Maybe when she's checking for lice, the nurse will see that Stephanie has the cooties, too," she snarled.

The Red Robins laughed. Alia glanced at me sympathetically from the next seat over. We shouldn't have sat in the seats closest to the Red Robins. We'd initially picked our chairs in hopes of absorbing some of Miss Brown's lesson but instead had gotten swarmed by Red Robins.

My friendship with Alia had grown into a best friendship, and I had the matching bracelet to prove it. Beyond the initial Barbie icebreaker, we'd bonded over mutual stories of overprotective parents, speech impediments, and in-school torment.

The teacher shushed everyone to listen to the rest of the morning announcements, which covered scintillating topics including bus number changes, a new policy outlawing slap bracelets, and some kind of tater tot situation.

"Alia," I whispered. "Do you think I have the cooties?"

She shrugged. "I dunno what they are. But I heard Stephen was sent away because he got 'em."

Stephen did not have the cooties. He moved to Florida with his mom after his parents got divorced. They pulled him out of school so suddenly his disappearance became linked to various child rumors, including jail, alien abduction, and getting recruited for Ed McMahon's Star Search. Today, cooties seemed the most logical theory. I was terrified.

Maria, a fellow Bo-Bo, couldn't resist chiming in. "You have the cooties if you wear the same clothes every day like Stephanie does."

I looked down at my clothes. I wore what Anyu gave me. I hadn't known, until now, that that was a problem.

Mohan let out a cackle, exposing a big gap of missing front teeth. He claimed to have lost them fighting a fourth grader, but everyone knew this was a lie because he was the smallest kid in class. He made up for his stature by making wise cracks at my expense. "You have the cooties when you have ugly brown spots on your skin like these," he said, pointing at the moles on my face from the adjacent table.

"Ew. You touched her. Now *you* have the cooties!" yelled Kiara. She skidded her chair away from him.

"Nuh-uh!" Mohan protested. "Last summer, my doctor gave me the Circle-Circle Dot-Dot Cootie Shot. Now I can't catch cooties ever." He stuck his tongue out at her.

I secretly scribbled down this cootie-prevention technique in my notebook with an orange crayon.

"Quiet down, class," Mrs. Pine ordered.

The morning announcements continued to drone on, but no one could hear them over the chatter.

"Alia probably has the cooties, too," Maria said. "I can tell because Alia and Stephanie can't say words right."

"Maybe they'll die of cooties," said Mohan.

I was equal parts upset about being made fun of as I was over the potential of having an infectious disease. I stayed quiet the rest of the day but burst into tears the moment I saw Anyu walking up the school parking lot. I blubbered nonsense during our entire walk home.

"Everyone says I have the cooties and I don't want to go away and die like Stephen. I need a shot from the doctor!"

I thrust a piece of paper into my mother's hands as though it were an official doctor's prescription:

KUTYS

Brown spots and if you wear the same clothes. If you can not say words right. Mohan can't get it he had dot shot in his arms.

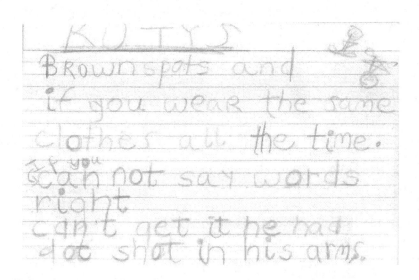

Handing her my notes was a bad idea. My mother launched into a complete panic attack.

"Oh my God. Did you put your mouth on the water fountain?"

"No!"

"Did you use someone else's sippy cup?

"No!"

"Did you shit down on the toilet?"

"Um. . ."

"Don't shit down on the toilet, Stephie. You'll catch disease!"

I continued to bawl.

"I can't handle it," she screamed. As soon as we arrived home, she called the school and hollered into the phone to anyone who'd listen. "Do I need to take her to the emergency room? Ve don't have insurance!"

The person on the other end of the line assumed she was upset about the head lice epidemic. They calmed her down and explained the lice checking procedure. As soon as Anyu hung up, she called Nagymama into the room and sat me down underneath the hottest floor lamp they could find. They hovered above me with a magnifying glass, pulling and poking at my head for what seemed like hours. If they found even a piece of lint, they put it on a piece of paper for ten minutes and watched it for sudden movement. Around midnight they gave up, and Nagymama made a late dinner. No one was hungry because they had images of creepy-crawly bugs in their mind.

I went into school the next day and the nurse examined my head with a giant mirror that made her look like she had a fish face. No lice. No cooties. Nothing. After the visit to the nurse, Mohan was immediately pulled out of class and remained mysteriously absent from school for the next few days.

I guess his cootie shot hadn't worked.

CHAPTER 11: TRICK-OR-DRINK

IT WAS 1990, the last decade of the century, and I was eight years old, nearly a decade myself. It was fall, the planning stage for the big event, Halloween. It's probably not shocking that I wanted to dress up as Barbie. Rather than buy a blonde wig and some type of princess gown, I knew we'd go to the local K-Mart and buy a Barbie kit, which contained what looked like a vinyl salon hair-cutting cape with a dress painted on it and a crappy plastic face mask.

Don't get me wrong. I wanted that cheapo costume because the other third graders ran around in vinyl versions of their own favorite characters. And it sure beat the heavyweight upholstery fabric my aunt used in prior years when constructing various couch-like costumes. Ever since a customer bailed on an order at Neni's upholstery store for a leopard couch in 1983, Neni found any excuse to make items out of this stiff, scratchy, gaudy material. Pillows, blankets, hot pants, and Halloween costumes were crafted year after year, until she finally ran out of fabric. This was the first year I'd be allowed to choose my own non-leopard costume. Vinyl Barbie was the clear and easy solution. Besides, Neni was busy preparing her own kids for high school graduation and college. For once, I thought, the whole family would be on the same page.

We went to the local K-Mart and purchased the costume. Aside from some minor distractions in the shoe aisle, the experience was fairly painless. I was excited, until we got home and Anyu whipped out a pair of trusty scissors. For a moment, I was afraid that it was time for my bowl cut. Instead, she dug the scissors into the Barbie mask.

Nagymama had to physically restrain me as I screamed, "Don't cut! Don't cut!" as if Anyu were amputating my real face. Convinced that the plastic mask would asphyxiate me, Anyu cut larger nostrils into the nose. In case my nose was stuffy, she cut off the lips. To prevent me from tripping, she cut open the eyes.

I glumly put on the tattered remains of my mask. At least Anyu hadn't cut into the dress. Of course, since New Jersey is a bit chilly on Halloween, Nagymama made me bundle up and cover my entire costume with my winter coat.

I went trick or treating with Anyu on one side, Nagymama on the other, waddling door to door, parts of my face randomly obscured by a jagged peach-colored piece of plastic, as though I'd slaughtered actual Barbie and was wearing her remains as a trophy. I wore two layers of patched-up sweatpants, a Christmas turtleneck, and a heavy, lumpy coat buttoned to my chin. I opened my coat to present myself to the neighbors, much like a flasher would do, if he first had to spend 15 seconds unzipping his pants.

The neighbors gave me wretched Mary Jane candies and stale Starlite mints to put inside of my McDonald's jack-o'-lantern Halloween pail, which had doubled as my potty years ago. Even with the stress and questionable candy circumstances, I enjoyed the transaction.

One of the stops on our Halloween route included Dimitri's house. As always, he invited us in. I hated going inside. His house always smelled like mothballs and smoke, and he and Nagymama would talk to each other in Dutch for hours on end.

This year was no different. We went inside. After a few minutes, I started to pace around the house anxiously. We were losing precious trick-or-treating hours, I thought. Dimitri's wife, Olga, hollered after me, "Shit down, shit down. You run around too much." I ignored her, thinking she bore an uncanny resemblance to Ursula the Sea Witch, though a much, much older version of the character I'd seen in *The Little Mermaid*.

"I get you something," she said and disappeared into the kitchen.

This scared me. Almost every other time I'd been there, Olga brought me hideously bitter grapefruit juice that Anyu would make me drink because it was good for me. I was thrilled when she brought out what looked like a cold glass of soda. I lifted my serial killer mask, took a fast gulp, and nearly spit it everywhere. I was expecting a delicious, syrupy glass of artificial flavor, but I got a mouth full of burning.

Nagymama was not pleased with the faces I was making. "Drink it. You don't vant to be rude, do you?" she said, giving me her menacing "Im'ona get the fakanál" stare.

I drank it. The family talked some more. Olga poured some more. Nagymama glared. I drank more.

At some point that night, their brand new Chihuahua, Peppy, came out. I dove behind Anyu's legs.

Olga found this hilarious. "Stephie, he von't hurt you."

"Anyu said I wasn't supposed to talk to strange dogs." I remembered the grisly pictures of dog attacks she'd shown me.

"Oh, Peppy is basically a cat."

I remembered the grisly stories and pictures related to cats. It wouldn't have mattered what animal she'd said. She could have said "Peppy is basically a hamster." Anyu had already indoctrinated me to fear all animals by telling me grisly stories and showing me photos of each individual animal tearing men asunder.

Peppy continued to bark. I cried. In an attempt to calm me down, Dimitri reached into his wallet and pulled out a five-dollar bill. "Hoppy Halloweenie!"

I jumped with glee, forgetting about Peppy and focusing instead on the thousands of pounds of candy I could purchase with five whole dollars. As I reached for the money, I got lightheaded and fell over.

The dog jumped on me. I screamed. Anyu screamed. Money flew across the room. Nagymama ran to catch it. Things were spilled. Olga laughed at us, presumably because this spectacle was better than anything she could watch on broadcast TV.

I was picked up by Anyu, ushered out, and brought home for fear of concussion. Nagymama deduced that I'd fallen because I hadn't been able to see correctly in my mask and had gotten my foot caught on my vinyl Barbie dress, and this was somehow Anyu's fault.

In retrospect, it probably had something to do with the two-and-a-half Black Russians that Olga had served me.

After Halloween, Anyu inspected my candy and threw most of it away because she was afraid of people putting dangerous substances in it. She never, not once, considered Black Russians a dangerous or hideously inappropriate Halloween treat for a child. So I didn't get much candy that year, but I did get to experience my first hangover.

CHAPTER 12: PEANUT BUTTER JELLY TIME

FOURTH GRADE was awesome. My teacher, Mrs. Giberna, discovered early that year that I needed eyeglasses. This simple fix improved my reading, writing, and drawing significantly. Her assessment changed my life.

That year, I received straight A's in every class, all four marking periods. I wasn't popular, but for the first time, I felt like there was a tiny little nerdy rock star inside of me, cheering and begging for an encore every time I finished a book. With books, I had the power to choose whatever fantasy worlds I wanted to live in, and I had the skills to draw those worlds and bring them to life. The book mobile became my second home.

On top of my improved academics, I was assigned the same lunch period as Alia. Whenever we could, we spent our entire lunch discussing our favorite colors (Mine: "glow-in-the-dark;" Hers: "hot-hot pink"), the cool stuff we wanted for our birthdays (a Game Boy and a Walkman), and girl stuff (Barbies, mermaids, princesses, in that order). Unfortunately, the lunch tables were in extra-long rows filled with dozens of kids. We often had to sit near people who were mean to us, especially our frenemy, Maria. Maria generally rotated from table to table and only visited us when she wanted something.

One February day, everyone was getting stir crazy from staying indoors because of the snow. Maria dropped her purple lunch bag on our table, clearly looking for trouble, conversation, or both.

"What the heck are you crunching on?" she said, inspecting my brown bag labeled "Stefike." She was always looking to switch lunches with someone because her mom always packed the same thing.

"Green peppers with margarine on toast," I said, trying to be polite. Maybe today would be the day we'd become actual friends. "What do you have?"

"Um, peanut butter and jelly, like normal people."

"Oh. I've never had that."

Both Alia and Maria's eyebrows went up.

"You've never had a peanut butter and jelly sandwich?" Alia asked.

Kids from the other lunch tables turned around. If for some reason there had been a DJ present, a record scratching sound would have been heard and the music would have stopped. If I wasn't uncool already, my friends had confirmed it.

"Listen," I whispered. "Peanut butter with jelly is weird."

Maria rolled her eyes. "Oh, okay, I guess fake butter with fake bread with weird wrong-colored peppers is more normal?"

I pondered while chewing. "My sandwich isn't fake. It's right here."

"Why don't you try a PB&J?" Alia asked.

"Yeah, try it." Maria split her sandwich in half and shoved the oozing concoction in my face.

I hesitated. Anyu told me to never eat food from strangers. Plus, her bread was weird and brown, not bright white like mine. What if Maria had crafted it out of dog poo and boogers to trick me, I wondered. As I watched her dive into her own half of the sandwich, I figured she wouldn't feed me anything that disgusting if she weren't willing to eat it herself. I took one bite and immediately spit it out into a napkin. I rummaged in my lunch bag, desperate for a juice box to wash it down.

"What's your problem?" Maria asked, shocked at my obvious abhorrence to her staple lunch cuisine.

"I don't like it! I don't like it!" I said, my mouth still sticky with sandwich residue. "The jelly slides over your tongue, the peanut butter sticks to the roof of your mouth, and just. . . . eeewwww!"

"Yeah, well, it's better than your weird Hungarian vegetable-butter sandwich."

Alia came to my defense. "I don't think there is such thing as a Hungarian vegetable butter sandwich. I think it might be British. You know, even though my Dad's from Egypt, my aunt and uncle are from London. Did I tell you about the time—"

"You guys are weird," Maria said, interrupting her. "I'm still hungry. I'm going to get school lunch. It's pizza day. You coming, Hungry-Hungry Hungarian?"

I shrugged. "I don't have any money."

She looked shocked. "That's okay. Neither do I." She held up a ticket that said, "Free Lunch."

"Whoa, cool, who'd you get that from? Willy Wonka?"

She genuinely laughed. "No, if your family is poor, you can get it."

"My family is poor!" I blurted.

"Cool," said Maria, impressed with me for the first time.

Maria showed me how to get the special paperwork for the free lunch program. I brought it home to Anyu and she instantly rejected the idea.

"They vant our social security numbers? They'll steal our identities!" Anyu said.

My cousin Erin was a young adult by this time and took pity on me. She helped me fill out the form and convinced Anyu to sign it. In the end, I was accepted into the program and Anyu was happy because not having to pack my lunch meant one less thing she and Nagymama had to worry about. With the free lunch program, I was allowed to get one free breakfast and one free lunch every school day.

It's shocking to me now, but the free lunch ticket was one of the few things for which I didn't get ridiculed. In a way, it was almost a badge of honor, a stamp that you were living a genuinely hard life and were not a spoiled rich kid. Because the school was diverse, there was a lot of racial tension, especially toward the white kids. The free lunch ticket was almost an olive branch. "Hey! I'm not snotty! I come in peace!"

Although I was eating more and more American convenience foods at home, it was of the fast food, McDonald's variety. Eating in the school cafeteria seemed exotic because I had the opportunity to try new foods like grilled cheese sandwiches, tater tots, celery with peanut butter and raisins (otherwise known as "ants on a log"), and chocolate milk. I was starting to assimilate and I liked it.

CHAPTER 13: MONA LISA

MY SCHOOL was closing forever. Piscataway Township made plans to combine the local elementary schools and turn my school into an administrative building. This meant that the teachers would lose their jobs. Ms. Hart wanted to end her Piscataway Elementary School legacy with an ambitious final project with her favorite class of fourth graders.

"Okay, class, we're going to have a little contest," Ms. Hart announced. She looked down the barrel of her paintbrush like she was looking through the scope of a rifle. "Girls who want to be in the contest, raise your hand."

A gaggle of girls raised their hands. She called on them one at a time and they lined up at the front of the class. I sank into my seat. She pointed around the room. "Okay, you, and you, and you, aaaaaand—" She paused, looking directly at me. "Why don't you join the group, Stephanie? Come up here."

I went from my standard nearly translucent pale shade to flushing beet red as I walked to the front of the class for evaluation. I stood next to the other girls, who were giggling and happy to be up there. Alia, seeing my fear, joined us at the front of the room as well. I felt better with her standing next to me.

Ms. Hart explained her idea. "I'm going to paint a picture of Mona Lisa, and one of you will get to stick your head through it. We're going to vote on who looks the most like Mona Lisa."

"I think Stephanie should do it," Alia said.

Gee, thanks, friend, I thought. She was probably trying to be helpful, because I always complained that I was never allowed to participate in anything artistic and additionally was picked last for gym class. I don't think she stopped to consider the social ramifications of busting one's head through a famous painting like Porky Pig at the end of a *Looney Tunes* cartoon.

"Uh, yeah," said a new girl from Pakistan. "Besides, she's the only white girl in the whole class."

A few people snickered, and I knew everybody was thinking it.

The class took a vote, and I was selected.

"Do you need me to do it for a photo or something?" I asked.

"Oh, no," Ms. Hart replied. "We're going to prop you up in the lunchroom during all of the lunch periods to make sure the entire school can see you."

"Oh, gee. I don't think I can do that. I have gym class during—"

"Don't worry. I'll get you out of gym."

I considered what would be less humiliating. Getting pounded in the face with an unending stream of dodge balls or tossed into a medieval torture stockade while painted to look like Mona Lisa?

I chose Mona Lisa.

Soon enough, I was sitting on a stool in the cafeteria, right next to children grabbing their chicken fingers and chocolate milk, smiling awkwardly through a crude imitation of a famous painting, attempting to replicate the most elusive facial expression in the history of art.

Initially, it wasn't that bad. Most people didn't notice me. Then, a first grader walked up to me.

"It is real?" she asked, as she poked me square in the eye.

I screamed; she screamed.

"The painting is alive!" she yelled, dropping her tray.

First graders who'd been previously ignoring me immediately split into two factions: the first ran from me in terror, and the second ran toward me like villagers storming Dracula's castle. Instead of pitchforks and torches, they wielded plastic forks and soft serve ice cream cones.

It was at that moment that the media showed up. Ms. Hart had sent out press releases to national arts publications, as if this were groundbreaking avant-garde elementary school art. The local newspaper was the only one to come out and cover it, probably as a fluff piece to soften the blow of the school closing.

"What a marvelous little girl in a marvelous painting!" The reporter shooed away the first graders and began taking thousands of photos.

Three lunch periods later, the ordeal was over. I tried to extract myself from the painting and discovered a massive amount of dried paint stuck in my hair, along with a decent helping of food that people had thrown at me.

Ms. Hart led me back to the art room to use orange-scented degooper on my head. It was the first time I didn't feel afraid of her. She was gentle, like Anyu when she washed my hair with baby shampoo. This teacher who'd scared me on a regular basis was going to go away. In a weird way, I was going to miss her. I was worried about her too. Where was she supposed to go?

**My dentist has had this photo hanging
in his office since 1992.**

I found out years later that she moved to a new school and kept teaching, which meant she'd found a way to keep scaring kids. I'm sad that I was never able to thank her for frightening us and for inspiring us to take art seriously. To me, making cartoons forbidden made them more titillating. I'd learned that art could change my life, not just via food-splattered humiliation, but also as a means to communicate when all other means were lost in translation.

CHAPTER 14: SAY GOODBYE

ELEMENTARY SCHOOL was officially over. I was moving on to middle school, and they were shutting down Piscataway Elementary for good. Being the last class to graduate felt like the climax of an action movie. We were walking away in slow motion, too cool to look back in our '80s sunglasses as the school exploded behind us.

On the last day of classes, I stood in the schoolyard with 100 other kids, all of us wearing matching teal-colored T-shirts with the words "Farewell PES" on the front. We sang "God Bless America" to our parents and teachers and got free ice cream sandwiches. As I poured myself a cup of lukewarm Orange Drank, the official drink of urban ten-year-olds, Alia walked up to me and said, "We're moving away."

I felt betrayed. We were supposed to be together, us against the world, until we graduated high school, went to the same college, and married twin Egyptian princes or lived under the sea or whatever the protagonist in the popular Disney movie at the time was doing.

There was one silver lining. We had one last summer to enjoy together, and we were going to make it count. We played together as much as we could, mostly in my backyard. Instead of playing Barbie Princess/Mermaid/Jungle Adventure, which was obviously kiddie stuff now beneath us, we concentrated on playing Barbie Boyfriend/Barbie Wedding/Barbie Gets to Use the Stove Adventure, like the big bad adults we thought we were. We were practicing for the real world — middle school — where we would experience kissing and dances and more kissing. We observed Barbie kiss transgender Ken doll, paying careful attention to the angle of her head and most importantly, what she was wearing during the kiss. It was unanimously decided that Ken preferred Barbie's authentic Mattel-Brand dresses to the pile-of-leaves-and-generic-brand-tape dress.

Insert your own choking-the-chicken joke here.

All this preparation was because we believed that when the school bell rang at our separate schools that fall, we were going to transform into beautiful women who looked like Barbie. Especially the part where our bones would shrink and our legs would grow to six times the length of our abdomens. To hurry along this process, Alia secretly took off her headscarf and put Sun-In Spray-In Hair Lightener Super Blonde with Lemon: Extra Tears Formula™ on her jet-black hair. It did nothing. I tried too, and it turned my whole head orange. Rather than resembling Barbie, I bore a remarkable resemblance to Ronald McDonald. Nagymama scrubbed my head violently with a bar of soap to "get the red whore out" and threatened to shave my head in my sleep if I ever tried that again.

Alia's father insisted that we needed to have more regularly scheduled activities so we'd stop ruining each other's hair out of sheer boredom. He and Anyu took us to the playground, where I watched from a distance as Alia conquered the Big Slide. Our families went to the shore together. I wasn't allowed in the ocean, but I could see it from a distance. We went to Six Flags Great Adventure. I wasn't allowed to go on any rides, but I could see from a distance that they looked like fun. Anyu let me go outside and I even got to eat a red snow cone. It was progress.

I don't have the dramatic memory that is in most movies of a moving van pulling away, with the protagonist running behind it as the best friend puts her hand on the window, desperate to catch one last glance of her friend before driving into the sunset. Alia's father scheduled a moving company and she and her family moved. She called me with her new phone number. I was sad but not hysterical. Even though we weren't in the same zip code anymore, we were still best friends.

Hearts full of childhood love, we hoped nothing would change.

CHAPTER 15: TRIAL BY FIRE

MUCH LIKE KINDERGARTEN, middle school had a rocky start. Middle school was across town, so I had to ride the big yellow bus. Although the bus stop was visible from our living room window, Nagymama insisted on walking me to it every morning because she feared I'd become the latest murder showcased on *20/20*. Being guarded by Nagymama was like being protected by Dimitri's Chihuahua, Peppy. She thought she was intimidating, but mostly the sight of her trying to defend anything elicited in strangers a mixture of laughter and pity.

I'd been one of the tallest kids in elementary school, the same height as my fourth grade teacher. Now suddenly, I felt small and out of place in this new environment of fifth to eighth graders, where the older kids seemed to know intrinsically where the classes were being held and what the electives meant. Some of the students had been held back a few times and were as old as fifteen. There was a girl on my bus who was pregnant, although I wasn't sure what that meant.

I felt ugly. I'd had a growth spurt over the summer, so I looked like an extra-dorky child jammed into a nearly adult-looking body, like one of those body-swapping '80s movies. Anyu was still dressing me in stained *Looney Tunes* sweatshirts and high water, patchy sweatpants. I wanted to wear makeup and dresses like the other girls. The only part of my outfit I was allowed to select were my eyeglasses, which I assumed were designer because they were the *Supergirl* brand. In reality, they were one of six choices available to kids receiving government subsidies for eyewear.

The *Supergirl* glasses, however, did give me enough confidence to strike up a conversation with Devi, a petite girl who stood at the bus stop with me. The first words I said to Devi were, "You look like Jasmine!" This was a huge compliment; I was referencing the most popular movie at the time, Disney's *Aladdin*. She half smiled and shyly averted her eyes, which were approximately 50 percent of her face. The effect was like a solar eclipse, so bright had been her gaze, and without it my own face felt dark and cold. But we were friends now.

For the next few months, while waiting for the bus, Devi and I patiently indulged Nagymama as she showed us her collection of Shopwise's "Have You Seen Me" missing children cards. After menacingly sounding out facts like, "Every 40 seconds a child goes missing in the U.S.," Nagymama quizzed us on the names, ages, and towns of the children who were missing. We rolled our eyes, discussing instead scented nail polish and glow-in-the-dark glitter eye shadow.

We assumed these kids had probably run away from their oppressive parents so they could go have fun. We were young, and we were invincible. We were obsessed with becoming adults, but we lacked the maturity to understand the gravity of a little old woman showing us a six-inch pile of missing children.

We were the last stop on the route. Both Devi and I were embarrassed when everyone saw Nagymama in her full curlers and babushka, shouting orders at me that involved anything from, "Don't eat anything they hand you!" to, "Remember to not shit on dah toilet!" The entire bus roared with laughter every time. But after the initial sting was over, everything was okay because at least Devi and I got to sit together and continue our super-important conversations.

I could tell that after a few months, Nagymama was starting to wear on Devi. Winter rolled in, and so did Nagymama's fear of winter-related death.

"Your ears too big," Nagymama said, grabbing the side of Devi's hair and pulling it over her ears, upset she didn't wear a hat. "Cold get inside brain, you freeze to death."

The next day, Nagymama brought her an extra, old smelly hat of mine and put it on her head.

"Thank you?" said Devi, stepping away, taken aback by the escalating personal contact.

Nagymama grabbed the bottom of Devi's coat and lifted it up to expose her belly.

"Jesus Maria. No undershirt! You'll get in-fucktion asthma. I bring you undershirt tomorrow. So brown! Which India? Dot head kind or corn kind?" She punctuated this last question with a Native American "Woo! Woo! Woo!" war cry offensive enough to belong in a 1930s Warner Bros. cartoon.

She was trying to be funny, I knew, but I was mortified.

The next day Devi asked to be transferred to a different bus stop. She never admitted that Nagymama's casual racism and winter attire assault was the reason, but I knew the truth. To accommodate Devi, a new stop was added to the route, more kids joined, and the bus was now officially overcapacity. I was still the last stop. After being laughed at over Nagymama's daily hollering ritual, I walked up the aisle alone, my head hung in shame. I prayed for there to be an absent kid so I could have a seat without being forced into a confrontation with bullies.

It seemed like the old elementary school bullies had informed the new middle school bullies that I was coming and to get ready. Perhaps the bullies had trading cards to identify easy targets.

Either way, I had a face that others could read like a book. My fear and discomfort were always on the surface, and the sharks fed on it. Devi sat in a three-seater row with two other shy kids. She didn't make eye contact anymore. My first middle school friend was gone thanks to Nagymama. I had no allies and no one to save a seat for me.

The bus driver, Daisy, yelled into the extra-wide rearview mirror, "We go through this every day. Somebody please make room for Stephanie!"

There was no room for me. With my backpack on, I weighed 130 pounds and took up the space of two average-sized children my age. I leaned a little too far to the left trying to get past a gauntlet of partially tied shoelaces and empty plastic barrels of fruit-flavored high fructose corn syrup.

"Move it, fatty. You're crushing me," said Kiara.

I walked towards the back of the bus and stood in the aisle, grasping the back of a seat in lieu of sitting down, as Daisy veered around the twists and turns of Possumtown Park. Suddenly, I felt a sting. Not like a bee. More like the type of sting you might experience when a much older kid puts out a menthol cigarette on your hand. Turns out that's exactly what it was.

I instinctively let go of the seat and fell to the ground. I smelled something burning. The floor was wet and left black marks on my pink sweatpants.

"White girls aren't allowed to sit in the back of the bus," Cigarette Burner said.

"But Rosa Parks said—" I stammered from the floor.

Cigarette Burner snapped, "Go sit up front with the Indians!"

I stayed down, deciding it was the path of least resistance. Even though my hand hurt, I wanted today to be the first day on the bus since Devi ditched me that I didn't cry.

"Get up off the floor or I will pull over and make a seat for you!" Daisy the driver screamed, slightly swerving.

"No one wants to sit with you. You smell," said Cigarette Burner's friend. She spoke into herself, making sure the cigarette smoke did not escape from her lungs inside of the bus.

Cigarette Burner laughed. "Yeah, why do you wear the same clothes all the time? I thought white people were supposed to be rich."

"Pshhhhh," said Burner's friend, blowing the smoke out of a cracked window. "White Girl's family is all vampires and witches. They spend all their money on sacrificing chickens and shit."

Daisy glanced in the mirror and noticed I was still on the floor. "Sit in a real seat or I swear, I will turn off the music and you will have to sit in silence."

The bus groaned. Listening to *Hot 97's Top 2 and Only 2 Playlist* was the highlight of everyone's morning.

I picked myself off the floor and apologized. I was sorry for being so big. I was sorry for causing a stir so the kids could not enjoy Ed Lover's morning show and beats from Doctor Dre. I apologized to the girl who'd burned me with a cigarette because my child-sized brain could not wrap my head around why a complete stranger would physically harm me. I thought I'd done something wrong. And I genuinely smiled when a couple of kids who were singing along to the music moved over half an inch for me. That was enough.

I awkwardly faced Kiara and perched my bottom on the tiniest possible part of the tattered brown seat cushion. I rested my elbows on my giant hot pink backpack and anxiously poked at the open cigarette wound. Kiara berated me for the rest of the bus ride, but I didn't care. Her words stung less than cigarette burns, and I was using all of my strength not to fall over every time the bus turned.

I could have and should have immediately asked to go to the nurse, but I waited until the end of the day when it was time for gym class. I'd endured enough pain and humiliation to earn an excuse out of my most hated school activity. The nurse asked who'd burned me and I told her the honest truth.

"I don't know," I said. "Older kids don't like me because I'm a cracker?"

The nurse frowned but said nothing.

Me on the Oregon Trail, just before dying of dysentery.

"I promise I didn't do anything. I'm too big for the bus. Can you send me a new bus?"

The nurse called my mother to tell her what had happened, but she didn't think the burn was bad enough to send me home from school. Back then, there weren't anti-bullying laws, stickers, and PSAs. The rule of the school was Suck It Up. I didn't want to ride on the bus anymore, not to school or back home from school, and I decided to find ways to miss it on purpose, starting that day.

When the nurse put me on the phone to talk to Anyu, I told her I was okay and that I'd be coming home on the late bus because I had club to go to. There was no club. I knew that the late bus was nearly empty and contained no bullies.

After the school day was over and Daisy's Cigarette Burning Bus left, I spent the hour and a half of free time drawing and reading comic books in the hallway. Without the constant noise of kids bullying me, my family criticizing me, or the buzz of television tantalizing me, I felt a new feeling: peace and serenity.

The only noise that accompanied the blissful magic hour that day was the distant sound of the janitor's sneakers squeaking on the floor and the occasional slop from his mop. It was me and pages of Rogue and Gambit nearly kissing and piles of sketches from "The Adventurers," an X-men rip-off comic I was designing.

The peace was interrupted by a dozen band and musical theater kids who were lining up to catch the late bus. I followed behind the flock, clutching my drawings to my chest in an attempt to become invisible, like the main character in my own comic book. It's sort of ridiculous that I was so intimidated by a bunch of theater geeks singing Whitney Houston love ballads at the top of their lungs. But I had no musical talent, and I was envious of their skills and sense of community. I assumed that they'd shun me. After all, most of them had been performing since age three. Their parents had purchased them voice lessons, dance lessons, piano lessons—the works. But then one of the girls, Crystal, sat down next to me and asked if she could French braid my hair.

I smiled through the pain of Crystal detangling my hair with a giant brush. I was finally included. As she slowly braided, I observed two girls swap bites of exotic homemade desserts from crinkly wads of tin foil. Another group of kids were teaching each other swears.

"Okay, so 'joder', 'chod', and 'diao'," said one boy.

"Does anyone else know how to say 'Fuck' in another language?" asked another boy.

"Fasz!" I exclaimed and reflexively prepared for the fakanál. "It's...Hungarian," I said, much softer, self-conscious again. The bus was silent for a moment. All eyes were on me.

"Hungarian? Cool!" the first boy said. "Do you know any more bad words?"

I knew many.

After the bus dropped me off, Anyu asked for a full explanation about my wound and my new French braid. Each seemed equally upsetting to her. She scolded me about the dangers of head lice and told me I was in need of a haircut as she poured peroxide and assorted unlabeled salves on my wounds. After she was satisfied that the wound was sterile, which I can only presume she calculated by the precise pitch of my screaming, she took me by the shoulders and looked me in the eyes.

"Stephanie. Don't tell anyone that the kids burned you. If you tell, they'll know and they'll burn our house down."

The next day, Anyu forced me to take the bus but provided me with a tiny first-aid kit in case it happened again.

Now I understand that as a child in occupied Transylvania, Anyu had seen friends and neighbors shipped to Siberia for simply speaking their minds. In comparison to that, a cigarette burn on the hand was nothing. She thought keeping your head down and packing Band-Aids was the smartest thing to do.

As a kid growing up in America, keeping my head down was not working. I realized I was going to have to find creative ways to keep the bullies off of my back.

CHAPTER 16: EVERYTHING I LEARNED ABOUT BEING A PROFESSIONAL ARTIST, I LEARNED IN FIFTH GRADE

I WAS ALWAYS good at drawing, but I didn't realize until the end of fifth grade that it would make an effective deterrent against bullies. People always found some reason to pick on me, but as soon as I started drawing popular animated and comic book characters, everyone, bullies included, gathered around to watch.

One day, Mohan, a now-humongous bully, spotted me at the drinking fountain. I froze like a deer caught in headlights as he came toward me. One of the reasons he got away with everything was because his mom was the lunch lady. He looked around to make sure the coast was clear before he talked to me.

"Uh, can you draw me a picture of this?"

He reached into his backpack and pulled out a weathered comic book featuring a big-breasted Amazonian woman with white hair.

I blushed. "Uh, I dunno who that is."

"Don't you know anything?" he snorted. "It's Glory from *Youngblood Strikefile*! I want a big poster of her for my wall. Like, life sized. Or bigger! Can you do it?"

I considered the logistics of the project for a moment.[1] Something told me that parents and teachers would not approve of this young

---

[1] Always consider logistics before giving a quote. Rule of thumb: (time it takes to make project x your hourly wages based on experience) + Materials + 10% contingency. Additional fees for rush jobs, "hazard pay," and travel.

lady fighting crime with her boobs hanging out like that. And if I didn't do the project well, Mohan would tell the other kids that I was a lousy artist, and the bullying would start again. I figured that if I worked after school before the late bus came every day for a solid month, I could create a great-looking poster without getting into trouble with my mom. But I would need resources.

I bit my lower lip and told him my price.

"Aw, come on, can't you do it for free? That's like three weeks allowance!"

"I don't get an allowance. I have to get paid making drawings so I can buy stuff."[2]

"That's weird. Why doesn't your mom buy you things? Oh, right, I forgot. Your family's poor." He laughed. His family was poor too, but Mohan's bullying style was to take emphasis off of his own deficiencies through diversion.

I blushed, put my head down, and turned away. "Well, okay, I gotta go now."[3]

He stomped his foot. "It's not fair. Why won't you do this? I can't draw, and drawing is fun for you."[4]

I turned back around. "Nuh-uh! I don't even like this character!"

"But she's popular. And if you make it good enough, maybe Disney will be impressed and let you work there."

"How's Disney gonna see the picture if it's in your house?"

He thought about that. "I have an uncle who works at Disney."

I considered this for a moment. "Awesome!" I said, furiously flipping open my sketchbook. "I have a bunch of my own ideas I want to show him, and maybe we can make them together."

"Oh, he's far away in Hollywood.[5] Come on, please? Are you gonna draw this for me or not? My mom will give you an extra chocolate milk at lunchtime for the next month."

---

[2] Yes, artists have bills too. Even in fifth grade.

[3] If a client is being abusive to force you to lower your rates, walk away.

[4] Commissions are not fun. It's called artwork, not arteasy.

[5] Beware of the promise of "exposure." Most people are full of malarkey.

Horizontal stripes match vertical stripes, right? Right?!

"My mom says chocolate milk makes you fat. And I can't trade chocolate milk for art supplies. I'm gonna need a lot of peach crayons to color all of this boob skin."[6]

"Wait a sec."

Mohan dug through his backpack and handed me a mangled box of dirty crayon stubs with a small pad of drawing paper. "There, now you can do it free."

---

[6] Bartering is good, but make sure it doesn't hurt your final product.

I looked at the powdery mess of wax. "There are no peach crayons in here, and the paper is too small."

"You can melt the other crayon colors into the one you need. Then you can glue the pieces of paper together to make them big."

"I'm not allowed to use matches. And gluing paper together looks crappy."[7]

"Fine. I have a thing of quarters next to my bed."

"That sounds fair."

Our complex negotiations were complete. The next day, he brought in his barrel of change. We counted every coin and it was still less than half of our agreed-upon price.

"Well," I said. "Maybe I can do a little-er picture."

"No way. I want the biggest picture ever! Wall sized. Can't you do it for cheaper?"[8]

"It's gonna take me a whole month to make it. I won't be able to make my own art projects or do drawings for other people that whole time, and I'm saving up quarters to beat *Darkstalkers* at the arcade."

"Well, if I give you any money, how do I know you're gonna finish it?"

"I have an idea," I said, doing math in my notebook. "If you give me the change bucket now, then you can pay me the rest when it's done. Like layaway or a deposit or whatever you call it. I'll make a receipt thing like they give at the store. One for you, one for me. And I guess we both sign it?"[9]

"That's a good idea. I'll get the rest from my brother. I'll tell him that if you ever become a famous artist, the picture will be worth a lot of money. And then you'll buy it back from us, right?"

"I'm not sure that's how it works. I think teacher said the value of art increases when the artist is dead."

"Okay, then we'll wait for that."

---

[7] Do not skimp on materials if you know if will affect the final product.

[8] With a limited budget, offer a mutually beneficial scaled-back solution.

[9] Clients and artists both benefit from a contract.

As expected, it took me about a month to draw the semi-pornographic poster in secret. I was constantly looking over my shoulder, afraid that someone might see it and take my barrel of precious video game quarters. The delivery day arrived and we met in the lunchroom by the trash cans.

"You got the picture?"

I pulled it out.

"Whoa. Her boobies are the size of my head!" He moved to grab it.

"Hold on a sec. Do you have extra money?"

"I forgot it. I'll bring it to you tomorrow. But I want to show this to my brother tonight." He made another grab for the picture.

"I think it would be better if you gave me the rest and then I gave you the picture."[10]

"Give it to me now," he said in a louder voice.

"Stop. You're gonna wrinkle it!"

Mohan's mom happened to walk by, donning her lunch lady garb.

"What is going on here?" she asked in a booming voice.

We both froze in place.

"Uh," we stammered.

"Give me whatever you are fighting about. Right now."

Her eyes grew wider as she unrolled the picture. I was terrified she was going to rip it up and toss it into the heap of discarded green beans and tater tots.

"You drew this?" she asked me.

I nodded but didn't look up at her.

"Why were you trying to take away her drawing, Mohan?"

"I paid for it, fair and square."

"Nuh-uh!" I dug around in my backpack and pulled out my copy of the receipt.

His mom looked at it closely.[11] "Mohan, this is your handwriting."

"Yeah, make her give it to me."

---

[10] Do not deliver your final project without your final payment.

[11] Sometimes involving a third, unbiased party can be helpful.

"Why did you lie to this girl? You don't have any money."

She dug around in her apron and pulled out a twenty-dollar bill. "Here you go, dear. Keep the change."

She turned to glare at Mohan. "I'll take some of it out of your next allowance. The rest you'll earn by mowing lawns."

"Aw!"

"Hey, if you buy something on credit, you need to pay for it, Moha."

"Mom! Don't call me 'Moha' at school!"

Mohan was miffed at me for about a week, but forgave me when his friends saw the blazing Glory art across his wall. He was the only kid on his block to own boobies the size of his head. Word spread and he was a hero among the fifth grade boys. One of his friends commissioned me to draw Rogue from the *X-Men* on his Trapper Keeper. (Her boobs were more reasonable). Much later, in high school, Mohan even bought a bunch of my weird ceramic palm tree lamps.

Of course, I was horrified when I discovered that the lamps were popular because they were easy to convert into bongs, but that's another story. Some of the bullies were off of my back, I had video game money, and I was officially an artist, a paid artist at that.

CHAPTER 17: THE SEGA SAGA

ALTHOUGH WE NO LONGER went to school together, Alia and I continued to speak on the phone, probably too much. She'd only moved 45 minutes away, which was far enough to keep our parents from offering to drive us to each other but close enough to be within a local calling zone. We made it within 100 feet of the dividing line between free and toll calls. Before cell phones, phone companies drew magical, arbitrary maps around calling areas so they could randomly ding you for ten cents a minute here and there.

I found this out the hard way when working on our French homework. Alia asked me to call her new next-door neighbor and classmate, Na'imah. The call to her neighbor, one house down, pushed us into a toll call zone, adding twenty-four dollars to our phone bill, a charge Anyu continues to guilt me about to this day.

We were bored tweens who looked up to terrible influences like *Beavis and Butthead* and *The Jerky Boys*. Whenever we had a snow day, we'd prank call the local radio stations, acting like mature adults until we went live on the air.

"Poop! Poopy poop poooooop!" we'd declare to the listeners at home while an announcer who was definitely not getting paid enough to deal with us sighed and hung up.

After radio stations figured out how to block our phone calls, we watched episodes of *The Simpsons* or played entire video games over the phone. Because I couldn't afford a game console, Alia would describe the game and I'd help her beat it. This approach did not work well for something like *Super Mario Bros.* ("Jump! Jump again, probably? Watch out for those mushroom things!") It worked great for adventure games.

None of our games had save points, meaning to win, you had to play them from beginning to end without stopping. For hours over the weekend, both of our houses were filled with incessant *Monkey Island* quotes like "How appropriate, you fight like a cow," and helpful *Maniac Mansion* suggestions like, "What happens if you put the hamster in the microwave?" This drove our families crazy. Without second phone lines, call waiting, cell phones, or the Internet, there was no way for anyone to communicate with the outside world during our video game marathons.

Alia's father broke down and bought me a Sega Genesis for my eleventh birthday. He was hoping that if I had my own game system, I'd stop calling Alia so much to play games over the phone. He would have been better off buying another phone line, but I wasn't going to complain. It was like receiving two birthday presents. I got a cutting-edge video game system and a visit from my friend, who I hadn't seen in over nine months.

The visit was exciting and confusing. Alia's voice was the same, but she was taller and seemed odd. When I asked her what was different, she proudly stated that it was her cool new training bra, a detail her father didn't appreciate her sharing. I filed in my brain that I should ask her about her exact training-bra specifications later. She poked fun at my Barbie cake, assuming it was Anyu's idea to get it. I was too embarrassed to correct her.

After blowing out the candles on my birthday cake, I acted surprised when Alia's father handed me the game system (Alia had spilled the beans about the present over the phone the day before). Anyu and Nagymama were genuinely surprised. Plus, they feared technology. It took Alia's father over an hour to convince them that the Sega could not record our conversations or ignite into a giant fireball if left plugged in for too long. By the time he set it up, they needed to leave because my birthday was on a school night. I hugged Alia goodbye but it didn't feel the same as last time. Who was this new person and what had she done with my Alia?

After they left, I cracked open *Sonic 2*, a game that came with the console. Anyu watched me play for a few minutes and didn't say anything. I peeked behind me and noticed she was smiling. I was excited that, at least for that brief moment, she approved of my actions.

Gaming meant so much to me, especially as a kid. Playing a game helped me explore new worlds, be another person, and do things that

I'd never be allowed or brave enough to do. I couldn't believe I'd gotten lucky enough to have something this luxurious, special, and magical. I didn't know how to communicate any of this to Anyu, so I looked over to her and asked, "You want to play, too?"

She looked genuinely shocked. "Oh, no, dat's kid's stuff."

"Come on, it's fun! You can play a fox with two tails."

"You know, Stephie, I vant you to think about something. Alia's father spent von hundred and twenty dollars on this video thing for you."

"I said 'Thank you!'"

"Your own asshole father vouldn't spend two cents on you."

"Uh-huh," I said, returning my gaze to the rambunctious blue hedgehog collecting gold coins.

"You need to start thinking about the future. Alia's father is a generous man. Maybe you should consider marrying him. Vhen you finish high school. His vife probably be dead by then."

When I told this story to my cousin Erin later that night, she laughed and said, "You're lucky you got a Sega dowry. Back in the old country, your mother would have traded you for two goats."

CHAPTER 18: PEN PALS

SCHOOL WAS OFFICIALLY out for summer, and I was looking forward to calling Alia to talk about the new Sega games I'd rented from the video store with the extra art money I'd made during the school year. I dialed Alia's number. Her brother, Seth, answered.

"Alia's at N'aimah's house," he said. "I don't like her. She's conceited. Hey, if you convert to Islam then you and I can get married and *you* can be here all the time instead of N'aimah!"

I was grossed out. Seth was Alia's annoying little brother and far from the man of my dreams, who I imagined to be Lestat from *Interview with the Vampire,* a book that was probably way too adult for me to be reading at the time. If the powers that be had their way, I could end up Alia's sister-in-law. Or stepmother. All I wanted to be was her best friend.

Instead of sleeping that night, I tossed and turned, imagining Alia's new bestie. They probably went to Mosque together, I thought, or rode camels through the desert and exchanged bites of kunafeh and basbousa. My brain went as far as imagining the two of them on a flying carpet together, but then I realized I'd seen *Aladdin* too many times and was being racist.

I knew I had to find a new best friend in case Alia forgot about me forever. It seemed like everyone in school had already paired off. You knew someone had a bestie because they often wore matching heart necklaces that had been split in half. For a while, I wondered why so many kids had evidently had their hearts broken by people with unlikely names like "BeFri" or "StEnd." Why commemorate that event? But after I saw the hearts interlock, it all made sense.

Finding kids with whom you had things in common was not easy in the early '90s. There was no Internet through which to instantly discover kids who shared your love of vampires, video games, and comic books. In order to nerd out with someone, I needed a pen pal. I decided to put my name, age, and home address into the Pen Pals section of *Wizard World* magazine. Anyu would have killed me if she'd known the truth. I told her the letters I received were part of some intricate summer school project.

"I vish men gave me this much attention," she said as she opened my letters to ensure they weren't full of bombs, poisoned candy, or porn catalogs.

Despite my terrible handwriting, I diligently wrote back to the dozens of sticker-and-glitter-filled letters from all over the world. The first letter came from Zsuzsa, a fellow tween Hungarian girl who liked *Batman* and ballet. She sent me a photograph of herself doing a beautiful, complicated stance in full ballet garb in front of an immaculately decorated fireplace. Wanting to impress her, I decided that I could be a ballerina, too. I cut holes into my socks to create makeshift leg warmers, put on a pink one-piece bathing suit, and had my mother take a photo of me imitating the pose in front of the radiator.

I never heard from Zsuzsa again, probably because she thought I was making fun of her. I may as well have scrawled in Sharpie, "This is you!" Years later, I stumbled upon this photograph. Realizing how perfect it would be as blackmail material, I ripped it into a thousand pieces. But the double-print copy I sent to Zsuzsa still lurks somewhere in Europe.

Then there was Kara, the daughter of a dairy farmer from Wisconsin. She liked playing video games and designing costumes for her favorite heifer, Dixie. Wanting to impress her, I decided that I could make costumes for farm animals too. I joined the local 4-H club and selected "sheep" as my farm animal. After all, my last name means "shepherd" in Hungarian. How hard could it be?

Coming from the suburbs and having no experience in animal husbandry, I was bad at sheepherding. I borrowed a sheep from one of the club leaders to practice on. The first time I tried to exhibit a costume at the county fair, my sheep pooped on it, became aroused when I tried to clean it, and then escaped. I realized I was a headache to everyone in the club after they started calling me "the fop with the rent-a-sheep." Although I had no idea what a "fop" was, it hurt my feelings because they said it in a mean tone. The dictionary said a "fop" was a 17th century British dandy, which confused me more. Had there been an Urban Dictionary instead of Merriam Webster, as there is now, I'd have realized they thought I was a city slicker, too sophisticated to know how to take care of my own sheep. Realizing that I'd changed my entire life so I could send cool pictures of myself to impress a random girl in Wisconsin, I stopped talking to Kara.

It was Thomas who caught my attention. He liked everything I liked: *X-Men*, poetry, and Anne Rice. He sent a photo of himself in wrestling gear, which intrigued me because it was probably the first time anyone athletic had ever acknowledged me beyond the usual gym class heckles. Wanting to impress him, I decided that I could learn about wrestling.

School had started again, and I was now in sixth grade. I decided to join the junior wrestling club as a statistician so I could understand Thomas's world better. That lasted for exactly 48 hours. When I found myself mopping blood and sweat off gym mats every day after school, it dawned on me that I was changing myself again to get someone to like me. I decided to try to be myself, for once.

Despite his interest in athletics, Thomas and I were nerds at heart, exchanging Sega cheat codes, comic doodles, and angst-ridden poetry. We played the world's slowest game of tic-tac-toe through the mail. (The "O's" were hearts. Cringe). We never thought we'd meet because both of our parents were overprotective, and we were too young to drive.

Then one day, out of the blue, my mother handed me the phone. "It's Tommy Boy," she said.

I grabbed the phone from her hand. "Ta-Ta-Ta-Thomas?" My palms began to sweat as I desperately tried to mask the stutter that surfaced when I was nervous. I'd given Thomas my real-life phone number in a previous letter, but I'd never expected him to pay long distance charges. For me! I couldn't wait to tell Alia. My immediate concern, however, was getting through the phone call without sounding like an idiot and without infuriating Anyu, who picked up the receiver of our second phone and sat with furrowed brows listening intently like an FBI agent monitoring a sting operation.

"My mom and I are in town. Can we meet tomorrow for lunch?" Thomas asked.

Anyu frowned and opened her mouth to protest.

"Our treat," he continued.

"Oh, really?" Anyu said.

There was an awkward pause. Thomas had no idea she was listening to our conversation.

"I mean, I know you'll be there too, Mrs. Yuhas, so I was thinking—"

"Yah, I always wanted to try the Sizzler at the Menlo Park Mall. We meet there."

Most of the bad decisions in my life I made while wearing a cowboy hat.

And with that, my mother officially pimped me out for a free buffet lunch.

The next morning, I tore apart my entire closet looking for the perfect outfit to make a good first impression. My idea of a good outfit at the time was a tossup between my oversized glow-in-the-dark vampire role-playing game shirt and my even more oversized vampire movie T-shirt.

"Vhy you always wear black? You look like death. Vear your pink dress. You'll look sexy," Anyu said.

The aforementioned pink dress was a frilly thing I'd made to dress up as Little Bo Peep during my sheep-costuming phase. I'd quit 4-H only six months prior, but it seemed like a lifetime ago. Overnight, the pink in my closet turned to black. Barbies became vampire novels. Strawberry lip gloss became black lipstick.

I eventually split the difference between Goth fashion and '90s fashion by combining mostly black clothes with neon bracelets and shoelaces. When she saw me, Anyu sighed. No one understands me, I thought, as we went on our way to my first date.

Thomas and his mother were waiting for us by the fountain. I recognized him from his photo before he recognized me. He was not as dark and brooding as I'd expected and not as crazy psycho-killer-y as Anyu had expected.

We hugged awkwardly. I was a full head taller than he was.

Anyu jumped in. "Isn't she a big girl? I always say, 'You too big. So big and pale. Like a ghost.'"

Thomas's mother politely laughed while I turned red.

My mother began to bombard his mom with questions: "How long did it take you to get here? Nice sweater. Vhat road did you take? How much did you pay for your sweater? Oh, you got ripped off. You should vatch your speed on Route 1, they have police trap. You should only look in the seventy-five percent off section; the sweaters are still good."

I was mortified, but Thomas saw the distraction as an escape opportunity. "Hey! The new *X-Men* is out. I hear this is the issue when Rogue and Gambit finally kiss."

"Really?" I stammered, afraid to look him in the eye. "I haven't heard about that."

His eyes sparkled mischievously. "Mom, we're going to go to the bookstore and grab a copy."

"Okay, dear," she said, looking tired.

"Don't cut your fingers up on the book corners, Stephie," Anyu said, turning back around to Thomas's mom. "So, how much you pay for property taxes in New York?"

Thomas grabbed my hand and dragged me into the store. My mind started to race. I hope my hands aren't too clammy, I thought, and why are they so big? Gosh, why is Anyu being so embarrassing? Why can't she drop me off at the mall like a normal person?

I was caught off guard when Thomas pulled me into the nonfiction section, put his hand behind my back, and dipped me.

For years, I'd dreamt about what my first kiss was going to feel like. I'd watched it in movies, studied it in comic books, and drawn pictures of it in the margins of my notebook. That first kiss was supposed to be an ethereal experience, filled with music and doves and. . . books about reptiles?

I barely had time to process what was happening before Thomas smashed his lips into mine, clanked his braces against my teeth, and injected his tongue as far into my mouth as he could. We stood in this pose for a second, me gagging, Thomas straining, neither of us knowing what to do. I'd heard of French kissing on TV, but I didn't think it would be so painful and weird. I certainly wasn't adding anything to the experience, being stiff as a board, my eyes wide open in sheer panic, afraid that my mom would walk in on us and punish me for the next four hundred years. To finish it off, he almost dropped me.

I did an awkward tango to regain my balance and saw spots as the blood rushed back to my head. In the end, it sort of felt like a wrestling move.

We had an awkward dinner at Sizzler. Anyu did most of the talking. I was afraid to make eye contact with anyone.

Can people tell that I've been kissed? I asked myself. Do I look different now? Why didn't it feel like it looks in the movies? Is Thomas bad at it? Am I bad at it? Was I pregnant now?

I wondered how long it would take for the baby to travel down my whole leg and out my foot like Nagymama said. I'm really tall, I thought, realizing it would take forever. At least I'd miss gym.

"Well, we should be going," said Thomas's mom. "Many more people to visit and we have a three hour drive back home."

Thomas gave me an awkward handshake and half hug. When his mom looked away, he turned around, smiled, and gave me an over-exaggerated wink on the way out.

"Well, they already paid for the buffet," said Anyu. "May as vell see if there's anything else?"

I nodded. I knew that Anyu wouldn't be satisfied until the lunch buffet officially rolled into the dinner buffet so we could pack up some of the steak in tin foil she'd hidden in her purse.

I spent the rest of the meal and the following week planning our wedding, which was different from the wedding I'd planned with Stephen in kindergarten. This time, I'd picked my mate myself instead of being plopped down into a kitchen with him and an oven baby.

Thomas broke up with me via the mail a week later. He didn't want to have a long distance relationship because he'd met a girl he liked. She was a wrestling statistician.

I was devastated. My first puppy love, my first kiss, a whole week's worth of wedding planning—all down the drain. I was sad, but there was a tiny glimmer of hope. I'd had my first kiss before anyone else I knew. Before Alia and possibly even before Kiara, Maria, and any of the other girls who were mean to me. Maybe I wouldn't end up needing to marry Alia's brother (or father) after all.

CHAPTER 19: FIRST BLOOD

ALTHOUGH I'D HAD my first kiss, I was pretty clueless when it came to sex, or for that matter, basic human anatomy.

I'd almost found out the truth early, at seven or eight years old. I'd seen a partially balled up, bloody maxi pad in the trash bin and run into my mom's bedroom, bin in hand.

"Anyu, Anyu! Who's bleeding?" I asked, waving the garbage towards her face.

"Oh. I sat on a nail at vork by accident," she said, wringing her hands and pacing around the room. "Now I bleed all the time, and I need a special tissue to catch it."

"Does it hurt?" I asked.

She grabbed the trash bin from me. "Don't tell anyvon, it's shameful!"

I'd believed her and forgotten about the whole incident. It wasn't until sixth grade that her little white lie became a big problem.

I was in shop. I'd originally wanted to take home economics in order to learn how to use a stove, but my mother had written a note to the teacher forbidding me from being allowed near an open flame. Apparently being around welding equipment and band saws was safer. We were making big useless metal key chains or something when I felt a weird, warm feeling on my seat. I stood up, looked down at the chair, and saw that it was completely covered in blood.

I hadn't sat on a nail, so why was this happening? I wondered.

I desperately tried to wipe the chair with a tissue I had in my pocket, but it made the situation worse. I looked around at the classroom full of students and decided to hide the chair in the back of the class under an old table between massive piles of scrap metal.

The teacher spotted my suspicious activity and walked over. "What's wrong, Stephanie?" he asked.

"Uh, can I go to the nurse?" I whispered while tying my jacket around my waist.

"For what reason?"

"Um," I stammered. I wanted to tell him, but I could hear my mother's voice in my head: Don't tell anyvon. It's shameful!

I made up some excuse and made the walk of shame to the nurse's office, clutching the sleeves of my jacket to my stomach. It was made of that horrible, early '90s ski-jacket material. It constantly slipped off and exposed my stain. As I repositioned the jacket for the hundredth time, I looked up and saw something pinned to the door of the nurse's office.

A note: "Out to lunch. Be back in an hour."

It was 12:15 p.m.

I didn't know what else to do. I walked over to the principal's office. Mrs. Deemie, the secretary with a heart of boiling evil, was sitting at the front desk.

"Can I help you?" she snapped, not even looking up from her paperwork.

"Um, the nurse isn't in the office and I have a problem."

"Well, then, you'll have to wait."

"But it's an emergency."

"What's the emergency?"

"Um." I looked around at the office full of administrators and blushed. I walked closer to her and said, "There was blood on my chair, Mrs. Deemie."

She glanced up at me. "Oh," she said, reaching around in her drawer for a second and handing me fifty cents. "Go to the faculty restroom and clean yourself up."

I was completely baffled by how fifty cents could help me with my situation, but I took the money and headed toward the door. As I reached for the handle, Mrs. Deemie proclaimed, "Oh, and Little Miss? I'm going to need to take your name down and what class you were in, in case you got period blood everywhere. Your seat probably needs to be decontaminated."

Several people turned around to look at me. My face turned redder than the seat of my pants. I filled out the form, awkwardly clutching my ski jacket and the fifty cents she'd given me in the same hand and scurried down the hall as fast as I could.

I entered the faculty restroom, praying for a miracle. I was hoping for a pants vending machine or vampire summoner or change-operated blood vacuum or something. Instead, there were the standard set of normal toilets and sinks. I spotted a vending machine in the corner with a sticker that said *50¢*. There were no other words or symbols, other than a picture of a cylinder thing on the left and a rectangle thing on the right.

I put the money in, turned the metal handle, and heard a click sound. I felt around at the base of the machine, jiggled the handle, and looked on the floor. The machine had taken my money and given me absolutely nothing. No cylinder. No rectangle.

It was at this point that I started to feel a bit woozy. I retreated into a stall to assess the situation. When I pulled down my pants and saw the volume of blood that had accumulated, I immediately turned to the toilet and threw up. After about fifteen minutes, I felt a little better. I snuck back to the nurse's office, but she still wasn't there. When the painful cramps kicked in, I was sent running back to the ladies room to wretch. I had no choice but to sit on the toilet and bleed out. Thirty minutes passed. Forty minutes. An hour.

I imagined a janitor or secretary finding me, dead, a pale husk of a girl in a swimming pool of her own blood. They'd hold a vigil in my honor and show my art. Nagymama would play the out-of-tune piano for six hours and everyone would cry and be sorry.

Tom Cruise as Lestat would surely perform my eulogy, I thought, and in my mind I could hear him speaking: "A great tragedy, Stephanie Yuhas, dying on a toilet that she once feared. If only we'd fixed the rectangle dispenser. Then this young girl wouldn't be dead!"

The click of high heels on tile interrupted my morbid fantasies.

"You okay in there?" a female voice asked.

"I think I'm dying," I whimpered.

Through her magnificent powers of persuasion, the teacher convinced me to come out from the toilet, made the secretary call the nurse, and found me a nice bed covered in exam table paper to keep me from messing up any more furniture. As I lay on the bed, clutching my stomach, the teacher stroked my hair and asked me an important question: "Stephanie, do you know where babies come from?"

"Yes," I said. "My Nagymama told me that kissing a boy puts a baby in your belly, then you get fat, and eventually you poop the baby out of the bottom of your foot."

Her eyes grew wide, but beyond that, she contained her shock well. She sighed, sat down next to me, and gave me a brief but graphic—and thoroughly accurate—description of the process. In the background, I could hear the nurse attempting to communicate with my mother on the phone. "No, she's not in any trouble. No, she didn't do anything. She's a woman now."

After an hour, my mom showed up with an extra pair of pants and a maxi pad the size of the Hoover Dam. I curled up in the back seat of our old station wagon, and we rode silently home. After taking medicine and napping for a few hours, I decided to get up and play Sega to pass the time.

My mom stood in the doorway for a minute, watching me play a game, then cleared her throat. "Stephie? I need to talk to you about something," she said.

I knew what was coming next. Most kids would have avoided The Sex Talk, but I wanted answers. Why had Nagymama and Anyu lied to me? What's the deal with this penis thing that people kept mentioning? Why do restrooms have tampon machines if they don't work? Also, what the heck was a tampon?

I was eager to learn everything. I paused the game and looked up at her. "Yes, Anyu?"

Anyu furrowed her brow, pointed at me, and said, "You get pregnant, I fuck you up."

Before I could open my mouth, she turned around and went back to her room.

I didn't know what to say. I went back to playing Sega. We never spoke of the birds and the bees again.

That day was the day I realized if I wanted answers about life, I was going to have to find them on my own.

CHAPTER 20: DRAMA

I WAS ZONING OUT in the hallway, obsessively flicking the tiny piece of Band-Aid that stuck out from the orange first aid kit I kept in my front pocket, when Crystal walked up to me. We'd been casual friends since bonding on the late bus, but I was never lucky enough to have classes or lunch break with her.

"Hey. Auditions are coming up for the spring musical. It's *Annie*. Are you going to try out?"

I was nervous about this. The only stage performances I'd been in were in choir, where participation was school mandated. A few years earlier, I'd been given a solo, specifically a Czechoslovakian love song. They didn't give me the part because I was good (I was not); I was the closest thing my school had to a Czechoslovakian. During the final show, I'd gotten nervous, forgotten the lyrics, and made up a completely new language and tune on the spot. No one had called me out on it, most likely because they'd been covering their ears due to my singing.

Even with my anxiety about public performance, the idea of having an excuse to spend more time with Crystal, the French-braider-extraordinaire, seemed too exciting to pass up.

I auditioned and got a part. It was Orphan #1, which was one step more challenging than Trash Can #2, but technically, still a part. Spending time with the drama club gradually started to crack my shell as a shy kid. Nothing helps someone get comfortable with public speaking, I learned, more than copious amounts of public speaking. Sounds simple, but I'd been living my life according to Anyu's old-world aphorism: "Avoid things you fear. Or else…The Revenge."

I'd gotten bit by the drama bug, so Crystal suggested that I get involved with the players' club at my local library. I was always looking for an excuse to see Crystal and spend more time at the library, so it was a win-win. Every Saturday I showed up to perform in some sort of production that involved public domain characters in public domain settings.

I'm not sure why I'm the only one dressed as a dog in this photo.

In some ironic twist of fate, I was cast as one of my greatest fears, a dog, in the fall play. I wasn't scared of the homemade dog costume Neni helped me make (I knew I wasn't going to bite myself), but I was scared when the neighbor's dog went into a frenzy when I practiced my barking. I was probably spouting all sorts of non-politically correct profanities in dog language.

I remember that I was practicing putting on my dog makeup in the mirror when Anyu got upset that Nagymama was taking a while to get back from the store. Once a week, Nagymama liked to walk to the local liquor store to pick up a lotto ticket. The store was a four-minute walk for an average person and a six-minute walk for a Nagymama-sized person. She'd been gone for one hour.

I stopped practicing my barks for a moment while Anyu called around. Nagymama was notorious in our neighborhood. All of the mom-and-pop shops knew her as "Babuska." The liquor store manager said she'd left a half hour ago, lotto ticket in hand. The clerk at the convenience store said she hadn't stopped by to pick up bread or margarine. She wasn't even at her usual spot at the local McDonald's, eating hamburgers and petting little kids on the head with greasy fingers while their parents smiled uncomfortably. Nagymama was missing.

We didn't find out until later that after purchasing her lotto ticket, she'd gone shopping for houses. Nagymama wanted a bi-level house, though she'd never spoken to a realtor and we did not have money for a different house of any type, not to mention one with more than one level.

Instead, she'd case houses in the neighborhood that were not for sale, I guess to purchase and presumably evict the current owners when she hit the lottery and became czar. Anyu and I told her that she shouldn't do things like this. This was trespassing and made everyone in the neighborhood uncomfortable. But nothing could stop Nagymama from walking onto people's front lawns and placing her cupped hands around her eyes in order to get a better peek into someone's personal space.

Usually, people would either ignore this or think it was funny. But she must have stumbled upon a new bi-level house with a jumpy neighbor. Nagymama was in their flowerbed, gazing into their downstairs bathroom, when the new homeowner called the police on her. They assumed she was an Alzheimer's patient who'd wandered off.

The police answered the call and drove up to Nagymama, asking her if she was lost. Although she spoke many languages, her hearing was bad and her English was still only so-so.

She lied in an extremely thick Hungarian accent. "No, no, I Mizz Mary Smith from New Brunsvick!" She had no identification on her, there was no car nearby with plates registered to "Mizz Mary Smith," and the town of New Brunswick was a fifteen minute drive from her location. Also, although she might have been the James Bond of Transylvania, in New Jersey she wasn't pulling off the identity of "Mary Smith."

The police also assumed she'd escaped from one of the local old folk's homes. Both police officers stepped out of the car and tried to get Nagymama into the back. They were trying to give her a seat in their police car so she'd be more comfortable while they called each facility to see who might be missing a small bearded lady resembling George Washington.

Nagymama thought they were arresting her. She clawed and kicked and scratched and screamed bloody murder. She punched one of the police officers in the chest. She screamed so loudly my mother was able to hear her from down the street. Anyu sprinted towards the noise. I followed her, forgetting I was in partial dog makeup.

There was such a commotion that the neighbors came outside to see the spectacle. My frenemy from school, Maria, along with her parents, three brothers, two sisters, and one zillion cousins, stood outside on their lawn. Maria was smirking. I wouldn't be shocked if she'd started a neighborhood betting pool on police activity revolving around our family. We knew how to disturb the peace and this was not the first time that Nagymama had a run-in with the law.

Last time, it hadn't been her fault. She'd been mugged on the same block because she'd refused to give up her purse; she'd been convinced the lottery ticket inside of it was a winner. The local McDonald's manager happened to be driving by. He saw a little old lady beating the assailant— coincidentally one of his employees—with her purse. If it hadn't been for him bringing the police by afterwards, she'd never have told us about what had happened.

Another time, a carjacker had run through our backyard and accidentally lost his Timberland boot in The Kapu. When the police showed up to claim the evidence, Nagymama specifically withheld it. This was her fault. They'd threatened to arrest her while she clutched the boot like Gollum, citing that it was her Men's size 14 hiking boot, and she'd lost the other one somewhere around the perimeter of the house. In truth, she was planning to resell them. To whom? I don't know.

The trespassing incident was the first time I saw her physically assault a police officer. Luckily, the police were gentle. Taken aback, but gentle.

"Officers, officers, dis is a mistake, dis is my mother!" said Anyu, putting her hands up to show she was unarmed.

Nagymama puttered to Anyu's side, took off her <u>papucs</u>, and started smacking Anyu as hard as she could.

"I knew it!" she yelled in Hungarian, "You called the cops! You're trying to send me to the nuthouse!"

Anyu was required to give a statement then and there. I provided translation for some of the big words. No charges were filed by the neighbors; they wanted someone to claim Nagymama and take her home. I was embarrassed, yet being involved in something official like this made me feel slightly important. The cops nodded at us and let us off the hook.

As we walked the half block home, Nagymama continued to scold Anyu for her alleged betrayal. I trailed back, not sure what to say or do. The neighbors started to trickle back inside their homes, except Maria, who called to Anyu.

"Hey! Is that your dog?" she said, pointing to me.

I'd forgotten all about the makeup and dog collar I was wearing. The police report must have been a big hit back at the station.

CHAPTER 21: SLEEPOVER

IT WAS EIGHTH GRADE and I was in the auditorium after school rehearsing for *The Wizard of Oz*. Through some miracle, I'd landed the part of Glenda the Good Witch. Maybe it was because my friend Crystal was the stage manager and she'd nudged the drama club advisor, who happened to be her mother, to give me the part. To me, this still counted as a miracle.

It was spring and we were only a few weeks away from show time. We needed to make costumes, and Crystal had a sewing machine. She invited me to a sleepover party at her place where we'd make costumes, eat junk food, and watch movies. All the girls were going to be there: Scarecrow, The Wicked Witch of the West, Dorothy, and her little dog, too. It was the first sleepover I'd ever been invited to.

I explained to Crystal that although it sounded exciting, Anyu would never allow me to go to a sleepover. I didn't mention that it was hard enough to get Anyu to allow me to go to a friend's house during the day.

Mrs. Zed, Crystal's mom, who was not just the drama club advisor but also a social worker, overheard us talking. She'd gotten to know Anyu through various school functions, and she had a unique grasp of my situation.

"Tell your mom you need to come to our house for rehearsal tomorrow. I'll invite your mom in for coffee and see if I can convince her to let you stay the night. We have extra nightgowns and toothbrushes if she says yes. At least you get to spend some time with us even if she says no."

This seemed like a fair and reasonable deal. Anyu brought me over the next day, partially because I convinced her that I could finally make use of that frilly pink dress she liked so much by turning it into my Glenda costume and partially because she was curious what type of house Crystal's family lived in.

"Are you a good witch or a bad witch?" "Mediocre, at best."

When I arrived, the girls were downstairs in Crystal's combination family room/craft room, putting the finishing touches on their *Wizard of Oz* costumes. A few of the girls ran upstairs and motioned for me to come join them.

"Come help me glue rubies onto the magical slippers," Crystal said.

"Hold on," I said, taking my time heading down the stairs. I wanted to eavesdrop while Mrs. Zed worked some real magic in the living room with Anyu.

I zoned out while they chatted quietly until I heard Mrs. Zed say sharply in a raised voice. "In order to further your daughter's development, I believe it is critical she spends a night away from home with friends her age. I assure you, she will be safe."

With those psychological buzzwords, Anyu was out the door. It was the most uncharacteristic thing she'd ever done. To this day, I have no idea how Mrs. Zed did it. Sorcery?

Exhilarated, I walked downstairs. The girls were dressed as their characters from *The Wizard of Oz*. Crystal was the only one of us who didn't need a costume so she'd bedazzled the words "Stage Manager" onto her black sweatshirt. It looked amazing.

"Here, Glenda, we made you a crown," Scarecrow said. She handed me a piece of poster board, also bedazzled. It was also amazing.

"Thank you very much!" I said.

This was so much fun, I thought, vowing to thank Crystal's mom someday for making this night happen. Maybe I'd buy her a bi-level with the money I was going to make off my Broadway debut as Glenda.

"Okay, now we're going to play 'Light as a Feather, Stiff as a Board,'" Crystal said, as she shimmied into position. The goal of this party game was to have a subject lie on the floor with her arms crossed over her chest while everyone else kneeled around her. Each girl would put her index and middle fingers underneath the subject, close her eyes, and chant until the subject floated in midair. The movie *The Craft* was popular at the time; we were sure this would work.

"Light as a feather, stiff as a board, light as a feather, stiff as a board. 1, 2, 3 and lift!"

"You guys, it's not working," complained Crystal, using the same tone she used when she was unhappy with our performance of "The Merry Old Land of Oz." "Dorothy, are you lifting with your aura?"

"Maybe your aura wouldn't be so heavy if you skipped chocolate cake," Scarecrow laughed.

"Light as a feather," we all continued.

"Hey, Dorothy! Is your sister asleep yet?" whispered The Wicked Witch of the West.

"Stiff as a board," we chanted.

Her sister, Toto, was curled up under an *Animaniacs* blanket.

"Yeah, Toto could sleep though a tornado," replied Dorothy.

"Me, too," I said, excited to chime in for the first time.

"Light as a feather," we repeated.

Our chanting was getting louder, and Crystal was getting lighter. Maybe it wasn't the chanting, I thought. Maybe it was our additional banter that was helping lift her. Inspired, I said, "I mean, gosh, don't you hate it when your parents shine a flashlight in your face to check your breath with a mirror every hour?"

The chanting stopped. I opened my eyes. Everyone had pulled their hands away from Crystal and was staring at me.

"What the hell?" Crystal asked.

"Do you feel lighter? I think you felt lighter!" I said.

"Your parents do *what* with a flashlight every hour?" asked Dorothy.

"My. . .my Nagymama. You know. She's afraid I'll stop breathing in the middle of the night so she checks my breath with a little mirror every couple of hours. Don't your parents do that?"

Stunned silence.

"Wow, now that is weird," said The Wicked Witch of the West.

I was the weirdest person in a room full of people dressed like low-budget *Wizard of Oz* characters, playing a game inspired by the occult.

I changed the subject as fast as I could by suggesting we watch a movie. Crystal picked *Rosemary's Baby.* The movie scared the bejesus out of us.

Swaddled by a sleeping bag instead of shoelaces, nuzzled by friends instead of chairs, knowing that no one was going to poke me awake with a flashlight and mirror, I fell right asleep. Everyone else, however, was afraid a Satanic baby was going to visit us. They stayed awake. I woke up only when I heard Crystal say the word *sex*. This was something I thought I knew about.

Since the period incident two years back, I'd started wearing headphones to bed, claiming they helped me sleep through Nagymama's snoring. Really, I was listening to Z100's *Love Phones*, a nightly radio talk show about sex. Health class at school was a joke. I saw this raunchy source as a perfectly valid addition to my education. That night, as we sat in our cartoon-themed sleeping bags in the dark, I taught the girls words like "sodomy," "cunnilingus," and "queefing." My weird naivety about bedtime procedures was water under the bridge compared to the knowledge I imbued into their innocent skulls. I was cool once more.

When Anyu came to pick me up the next morning, I couldn't help but look at her differently. Why are you letting Nagymama continue the bedtime ritual if it's not normal? I almost asked her, but I didn't because I was afraid she'd think my friends were a bad influence on me and not let me go to sleepovers again.

I thought it would be safer to call my lifeline, my cousins, and ask what they thought. Erin answered the phone.

"Oh, my gosh. Your mom and grandma were terrified that you would die of SIDS, you know, sudden infant death syndrome? They heard about it on the news, and they started checking your breath with a mirror when you were a baby. They still do it?"

"What?" Irina asked as she picked up the other extension. "Why don't you stop them?"

"I don't know," I said. "Nagymama's hearing is so bad these days that she doesn't even hear me when I protest. Besides, they tie me into bed so tight that it's hard for me to move and fight back when she does it."

"What?" Irina said. "That's insane."

"You know Nagymama," Erin said. "She's probably afraid that Steph will catch a cold or infection."

"But the mirror? You're almost in high school!" Irina continued. "What would she even do if Stephanie stopped breathing one day?"

Erin laughed. "You should mess with them. Like, hold your breath and see what happens."

It was a plan I'd never considered, but I couldn't shake the idea from my brain.

The following afternoon, I drank way too many slushies and needed to use the bathroom in the middle of the night. But I was packed into bed.

"Nagymama."

She snored loudly.

"Nagymama!" I yelled and waited.

Another big snore.

Ten minutes later, she woke up, apparently for reasons unrelated to my screaming, and started muttering. She felt around in the dark for her flashlight and clicked it on. She muttered about a man who'd come to her house in 1970 and asked her to order a pepperoni pizza. She looked for her papucs.

One foot. Two feet. She sauntered over to me. She muttered that the man did not offer her a glass of water when she went to his house.

She leaned over to check my breath with the hand mirror. She muttered that the man was selfish because she did, in fact, purchase him a pepperoni pizza.

I was about to ask if she could untie me so I could use the bathroom. Then I remembered what my cousin said. Feeling belligerent, I held my breath.

For the next minute, Nagymama ran around the house screaming. Anyu ran into the room, with equal parts panic and unhelpfulness. At one point the bottle of holy water was retrieved and splashed on my face. Yet, did either of them think to call an ambulance, administer CPR, or even check for a pulse?

It wasn't until they started discussing how to make my death look like it was an accident and how they would explain it to the police that I started laughing out loud. They released me from my bed sheet prison to give me a good beating with the fakanál, but I was bigger and stronger than the both of them by this time. I stampeded over them so I could run to the bathroom and relieve myself.

Nagymama never checked my breath with a mirror again. I'd won the battle, but the war was still raging.

CHAPTER 22: SECRET SHOWER

NAGYMAMA FELT that Americans bathed too much. She believed excessive baths led to red hair (which made you look like a whore), hair loss (at least it wouldn't be red anymore), and kidney infections (the final step before the grave).

Consequently, I was only allowed to take a bath once a week. Showering was forbidden. Nagymama claimed that standing in the shower would expose my organs, despite them being well wrapped in pounds upon pounds of muscle and flesh, and give me pneumonia. "Ve don't have insurance!" she'd remind me for the millionth time.

I was fourteen, getting ready to graduate from eighth grade, and I had Jamar, my steady boyfriend who went to high school. We made out at the movie theater sometimes, so I was concerned about hygiene and personal grooming. But I had to wait until Nagymama fell asleep to wriggle out of my bed—I was strong enough to do that these days—and try to shave and shower.

If Nagymama woke up and noticed I was missing, she'd start screaming and banging on the bathroom door. I'd have about two minutes to finish the shower before Nagymama picked the lock, barged in like a stampeding wildebeest, and pulled me out of the shower—naked, soapy, and incredibly pissed off. Then she and Anyu would take turns blow-drying my hair for over an hour until it was the consistency of scorched tumbleweed. Sometimes I cried because the experience was physically painful.

"It's for your own good so you don't die," Nagymama said.

I was older now and a tiny bit wiser. I tried to look at it from their perspective. Their love was a smothering kind of love, the kind that binds you, protects you, and leaves you with heat rash. I thought the most peaceful way to handle their hysteria was to sneak around, not make waves, and try to gasp small breaths of freedom without them noticing. But they always pulled me back under and pushed me down farther.

The only thing showering did not lead to was crimped hair. The '80s were to blame for that.

Also, something niggled me about the routine. I couldn't figure out how Nagymama, an elderly, hard-of-hearing woman, woke up whenever I tried to shower. She also woke up every time I tried to sneak out of the house in the morning in an attempt to have at least one drama-free day at the bus stop. Did Nagymama have radar? I wondered. Was it a spooky third eye thing?

Anyu couldn't understand it, either. "I guess you vere too loud," she'd say. "Dat old bitch is up and you've gotta deal vith her now!"

One night, instead of sneaking out of my bed and heading directly to the bathroom, I hid around the kitchen corner. And like that, the elusive answer to this long-time mystery revealed itself.

I witnessed Anyu get up, tip toe over to Nagymama's side of the bed, and violently shake her. "The child is awake," she whispered in Nagymama's ear. Then Anyu sent her to the bathroom to get me while she went into the kitchen to fix herself a midnight snack.

I felt hurt and used. I could not understand Anyu's behavior. Wouldn't it have been better to let Nagymama sleep so we could go about our business every once in a while? Did we need to start every morning and end every night with kicking, screaming, and hitting?

"Why did you do that?" I accused Anyu from my hiding spot in the hallway.

Anyu jumped. She had no idea I was hiding there. I continued to yell at her, demanding answers for her betrayal. She stared at me blankly while Nagymama grabbed me by the elbow and dragged me back into the bedroom. Caught in a lie, Anyu had powered down like a robot. I stopped struggling and turned my head to look at Anyu one last time as Nagymama tied me into bed. Anyu was still standing there, in the kitchen, in the same spot. Silent. Unmoving. Broken.

* * *

The final straw came one night when I was already in a foul mood because I had terrible cramps and a disgusting day at school. A starfish had ejected his stomach before making some bad starfish life choice that got him captured, killed, and pinned to my dissection table. I wanted to take a shower to wash the formaldehyde-y memories from my body and mind. I had to formulate a plan. I grabbed a roll of duct tape and a small chair from the garage and hid it in the one place they would never look—the shower.

After Nagymama fell asleep, I wiggled out of bed, snuck in the bathroom, pulled out my tools, and barricaded the bathroom door shut. Anyu went through her usual tattletale ritual, and Nagymama started knocking.

"No shower vhen you on dah rag, Stephie," she yelled through the door. "You vill bleed to death!"

While I took my clothes off, I heard her rummaging around her key box to try to find her lock pick, which of course, is a perfectly normal go-to tool that most grandmas have. I could hear her gasp when she realized it was gone. I smiled; I'd brought it into the bathroom with me. I hummed to myself for being so clever and turned on the shower as she scuffled around outside, screaming, cursing, and attempting to bust through the door with her shoulder.

Silly Nagymama, this isn't some special babushka-lady episode of *Cops,* I thought, reaching for my secret ladies' razor to shave my legs. My family had forbidden me from shaving because they said my hair would grow back thicker. They didn't even let me have a pair of tweezers because I was a stupid child who couldn't be trusted around sharp objects. I'd hidden my razors, tweezers, and general sharp objects in my sack of old Barbie dolls.

As I was bending over to shave my legs, I heard a terrible crash and felt a gust of cold air. The noise startled me so much that I cut right into my knee. Nagymama ripped the shower curtain off of the rod. She'd taken the door off the hinges.

She pointed to my bleeding leg. "You see," she screamed. "Showering on dah rag makes you bleed to death!"

As punishment, Nagymama said she was taking the bathroom door away forever. Anyu did not argue. She just stood there.

Growing up, I'd thought we were quirky, and later I'd realized we were weird. Now I was beginning to see our relationships were borderline abusive.

Over the next few months, I begged Anyu to move out with me so we could leave the house and Nagymama behind. Anyu always said nothing.

Maybe it was Stockholm syndrome. She'd chosen Nagymama over two husbands and now she was choosing her over me.

I was making my choice, too. I was planning my escape.

CHAPTER 23: HIGH SCHOOL

THE FIRST TIME I walked through the doors of Piscataway High School, people moved to the side as I passed through the hallways. Whispers from the rumor mill had circulated around the school before I'd even enrolled. Jamar, my boyfriend, had whipped out his penis at a Labor Day barbeque. There I was, getting a veggie dog, and all of a sudden: Penis! Yay?

"How about this hot dog?" Jamar said, proudly showcasing his junk.

Did he want me to apply mustard to it? I wondered.

I'd never seen a penis before, let alone a surprise penis, so the face I made was probably not great for his ego. Serves him right. He knew my thoughts on the subject. In fact, we were both wearing abstinence rings when it happened.

"Gosh, I thought you'd be excited," he said, "You can still be a virgin and touch dicks. After five months, if the girl doesn't go for it, the guy is allowed to whip it out."

Clearly, I thought, that must be chiseled on a stone somewhere.

"Uh, I gotta go," I said. "Thank you for...your time. And the barbeque. Hot dog."

We'd broken up over the phone the next day. To save face, he'd contrived a myth that I was a prostitute who drank people's blood for money. My accent was gone, but the Dracula legend remained. In a way, Jamar did me a favor because not as many people messed with me in high school. "Wiccan Vampire Slut" sounded more intimidating than "Christian Vegetarian Virgin." I guess I did dress a little Goth.

It didn't matter. I was a woman on a mission. I needed to spend as much time away from my house as possible and figure out a way to leave it for good. I received a brochure in the mail for The University of the Arts, based in Philadelphia. On the cover was a poster, a picture taken of hundreds of students, the prior year's graduating class, smiling and shouting, holding up whimsical blow-up pretzels and funny paintings. On the back, they listed a major I'd never heard of: Animation.

I could go to school to make cartoons? And earn money doing it? I should be ashamed of what a victim of marketing I was to fall for this propaganda, but the program sounded like a dream come true. There was only one problem. It cost $80,000. I had to get a scholarship.

I was an A and B student and had dabbled in a little bit of theater, but in high school, I stepped up my game to become an academic and elective junkie. I took all of the honors and AP classes. I became a social chameleon, seeking out any non-athletic clubs, cliques, and groups I could infiltrate with the least amount of commotion.

My old favorite, the Drama Club, was out of the question because it required full-time commitment and one of my schoolmates played Rudy Huxtable in *The Cosby Show*. No use in trying to compete with perfection, I figured. Plus I was getting too old for the players' group at the local library, and I assumed "Director of *Duck-Duck-Goose: The Musical*" wouldn't look that impressive on my college resume.

I joined Honors Society and Student Government, but they both felt like popularity contests, and I wasn't taken seriously. I contributed angst-ridden poetry to the Literary Club even though it made me feel pretentious.

I volunteered for Key Club, where they instructed me to go door to door with a little orange box to raise money for iodine deficiency disorder. No one gave more than a quarter. I hated the constant random interaction with strangers. After all, weren't strangers dangerous?

During family dinner one night, I noticed that McDonald's had iodized salt packets. Thousands of them. I filled my orange box and my pockets with salt packets and then sweetly asked the Key Club proctor to put them in the box going to Africa. I was proud of this scheme. If we convinced everyone in Key Club to do this, we could single-handedly stop the world's goiter problems. Why hadn't anybody else thought of this?

I'm pretty sure the proctor promoted me to editor of the Key Club so I would be kept busy making terrible clip art newsletters and no longer have time to contribute helpful fundraising ideas.

**Oh my Goth. It's so hard to
look brooding in nice
weather.**

Still, that title snagged me a position as art editor of the school
newspaper. I had fun at first, successfully designing dozens of issues. I
skipped the clip art and opted for original commissioned art, so I started
to make some friends in the art department. I even got my own satirical
advice column in a special April Fools' Day issue. The shtick was an
advice columnist who gives ridiculous, unhelpful answers to basic
problems with obvious solutions. Right before going to print, the editor
of the paper gave my column the spoof headline, "Stephie Gives Advice
to Those That Have No Life."

"Get it, Stephanie?" he said. "They have no life? Because they aren't
real? Har har har."

No one read past the headline or got the joke. One person accused
me of offending a friend of his who wrote in for help, even though all of
the questions and answers were satire, written in one night, by me

AMERICAN GOULASH   127

and only me, after drinking way too much Jolt Cola. It was only printed because I failed to sell a remnant piece of ad space before our publishing deadline.

The worst club offender was likely my participation in S.C.A.R.E.D. (Students Concerned About 'R' Environment's Destruction). Despite the terrible acronym and abundance of worm-related activities, my favorite science teacher ran the program and I loved being around him. He was positive, energetic, and funny, a father figure I looked up to and admired. He convinced me to don a spandex jumpsuit and become Recycle Girl. He dressed like Ant Man and we fought in the school cafeteria. I guess Ant Man didn't recycle? I don't remember. Every time I endured another public humiliation like this for the sake of resume material, I looked at the University of the Arts poster.

Years of drawing comics culminated in my grand opus, "Alarmo, pas en repos" ("Alarmo, Not in Repose," 1997).

My plan was working. I was that annoying freshman in the back row, center of every single club yearbook photo. I was taking the late-late bus and arriving home at 5 p.m., just in time to go to my new part-time job working at a call center to sell Slomin's Shield Home Security Systems. I showed up on time, was cooperative, and made awesome window murals at holiday times. But I was so bad at selling alarm systems they had to promote me to data entry because they didn't want to fire me. I was getting good at climbing the professional ladder by sucking at things.

On weekends, I taught crafts to children at Vacation Bible School and did filing in the church's main office. Every moment of every day was school, work, art, eating, or sleeping. As long as I kept myself busy, I didn't have to think about the increasing conflict at home and I could ignore the occasional whispers about my alleged sluttiness in the halls. I was also bringing in real money for the first time. I could help with some of the basic necessities around the house and save a little extra for a used car for my escape.

I was perfectly fine with my distractions until the week before Valentine's Day my freshman year of high school. I had no valentine. I liked it better in elementary school when everyone was required to give a Valentine's Day card to everyone in his or her class. In high school, there was a new rule, namely that whoever did not get a carnation or gifts on Valentine's Day was human garbage.

I would have been happy to get a carnation from anyone, but my real hope was that I'd get one from George, the adorable blond boy I ran into during my 2-D art class and Art Honors Society meetings. His passion and talent for art only fueled my crush. I'd initially promised myself that I wouldn't let myself get distracted by boys. I'd focus on work so I could get into and pay for art school. But date an art boy? We could be twice as productive!

I never had the guts to say anything to him other than, "Have you seen the rubber cement?" Usually, I'd blush and run away before George even replied. Poor confused George was probably sitting there, grasping rubber cement he didn't need, wondering why he'd gotten oddly pranked by a Goth girl.

I was internally lamenting about my singleness when Tiffany, one of the most popular girls in high school, plopped herself down in the seat next to me. Tiffany had a perfect attendance record so she was a hit with the teachers. She did a ton of charity work so she was a hit with the parents. She was athletic so she was a hit with the cheerleaders. And she developed gigantoid boobs when she was eleven so she was a hit with the boys. Normally, girls like Tiffany ignored me, but I still had one thing going for me.

"This drawing sucks. I need your help," Tiffany said as she showed me a cartoonish picture of her and a boy, smooching inside of a big heart surrounded by cupids and bears.

"The problem is you're using your fingers to blend the colors. The oils from your skin are smearing everything."

I gave her a fancy-shmancy paper tortillion that I'd spent eighty-nine whole cents on. I'd received a raise at work so I was the Daddy Warbucks of the art supply store.

"Oh, you're such a lifesaver. Jeremy is going to love this when I'm done. I'm making this as a part of his Valentine's Day present."

"Uh-huh."

"I think it's totally crappy that guys are always expected to be the romantic ones. This year, I'm going to spoil him—buy *him* flowers, buy *him* candy."

"Uh-huh."

"And everyone knows, no Valentine's Day gift is complete without a handmade card. And maybe a teddy bear. I don't know. Is that too girly? Are you buying your boyfriend a stuffed animal?"

"Oh. No, I don't have a boyfriend."

"Seriously? Well, got a crush?"

My eyes unintentionally darted over to George.

"Oh my gosh, you like George?"

"Shhhh, he'll hear you!"

"You should ask him out. We're friends. He's totally single."

"Please don't say anything. He doesn't even know I'm alive."

"You need to stop waiting for men to come to you. Be a little more aggressive. Woo him. It worked for me!"

Tiffany and I took the rest of the period to devise an elaborate scheme to win George's attention. Tiffany's first step was a complete makeover. I wasn't allowed to wear makeup, and my mother forbade me from wearing skirts in winter (see: "kidney colds"). I convinced Crystal to help with my latest ploy. Over the next few days, we altered a couple of my old choir uniforms to look like Alicia Silverstone's clothes in the movie *Clueless*.

For the entire week, I snuck what I perceived as cute and completely appropriate outfits to school and changed in the bathroom. Tiffany would meet me in there, heaving my large body into thigh-high stockings that never fit me correctly, styling my hair, and doing my makeup.

Despite my best efforts, George didn't give me a second glance. The only man taking notice of this style shift was the principal of the school, who cited me for wearing skirts that were way too short and made me change into my gym clothes. It seemed like I could never run into George when I looked cute, but he was always right beside me when I was sporting my homemade *Star Trek IV* T-shirt that proclaimed "Admiral, Thar Be Whales Here."

"Stephanie, if you ever wear that T-shirt again, I will throw it into the ocean where it belongs," Tiffany said, as she shoved a piece of paper into my hand. "38-24-34."

"Your measurements?" I asked.

"No, stupid," she whispered into my ear. "It's George's locker combination."

"*What?* What do you want me to do with it?"

"Something romantic! You should totally go buy some flowers or something and stick them in his locker tomorrow so he'll have them on Valentine's Day. He'll be so impressed with the amount of effort it took you to sneak them in, he'll go out with you for sure."

I was fairly confident that this plan would work. It was reminiscent of the stories I'd read about in trashy romance novels and those "How to Meet the Love of Your Life" blurbs in our local paper. I deduced that I could start a real love advice column in our school newspaper based around the imminent success of my scheme.

The next day, I bought fifteen dollars worth of Mylar balloons, some roses, and a dorky little teddy bear. I agonized with the shop clerk over the inscription on the card. Whatever we decided on, it was not good. All I can bear to remember is writing my name, phone number, and the extremely helpful detail, "You know, the girl with the brown hair."

I had fifty cents left over. As a reward for my bravery, I purchased myself a strawberry cheesecake lollipop. It was only after I opened the wrapper that it dawned on me: I had George's locker combination, but I didn't know which locker was his. I scrounged around for change to use the pay phone, but I'd spent my last dime on George's Valentine's Day present. I begged the clerk to refund my lollipop. He glared at me and shook his head. Still, he grabbed the lollipop out of my hand, threw it into the trash, and silently slid the fifty cents back to me.

"Thank you!" I called as I bolted out of the front door toward the pay phone in the courtyard. I struggled to walk across campus. My heavy backpack, my armful of Valentine's Day supplies, and my tiny skirt that day each posed major hazards during my journey. In the phone booth, I did a clumsy shuffle, placing the flowers and bear between my legs while I flipped through my trapper keeper full of phone numbers and balanced the disgusting public phone in the crook of my neck.

"Hello?"

"Ta-Ta-Ta-Tiffany?" The wind had started swirling a dust of snow around me, chilling me to the bone.

"Yes?"

"It's Steph. I—"

"Oooo! Did George ask you out?"

"Na-na-na. No. I don't know his locker number."

"What? I gave it to you!"

"No...the *number* of the locker."

"Oh! Hold on, girlfriend."

I glanced down to see what was hurting my knee. The roses had pieced through their plastic wrap container and were stabbing me in the leg.

"Shoot-" I nearly dropped everything and lost the balloons trying to recover.

Tiffany returned with the magic numbers. "Uh, it's 1141. Make sure you pull hard; George is always fighting with that thing. It sticks."

"Okay. Fine. Thanks. Bye."

I threw the phone back onto the cradle and ran to the girls' bathroom. I dropped everything on the floor and assessed the damage. The thorns had stayed attached to the flowers but managed to pierce my skin enough so that the right ear of the white teddy bear was stained with blood. I immediately dunked the bear's ear into the sink to scrub him clean. Kiara, my archnemesis since elementary school, came out of a stall and gave me the stink eye. I tried to ignore her as I cleaned up my wounds and dried the bear's head under the hand dryer.

I went over to locker 1141, looking over every last inch of the Valentine's Day gift to make sure there was no forensic evidence on it. I entered the combination and...nothing. I tried again and heard a click, but the door wouldn't budge. I pulled and pulled until a kindly janitor walked by.

"Here, let me help you," he said. He pulled out his keys and popped it open. A ton of sheet music fluttered out of the locker. "If yah keep shovin' dese tings in the locker, your locker will keep jammin'."

As soon as he turned his back, I threw the sheet music into the locker, shoved the Valentine's Day gift in there, and slammed it shut. I took the late bus home and didn't utter a word about my plan to another soul.

That night, I barely slept a wink, imagining George's reaction to my gift. I wondered what the sheet music was and if George would ever play me a song. I wondered if he'd sing this song at our wedding.

The next day, I woke up to what I thought would be my new life, together with George.

"Go back to sleep," Anyu said. "Is a snow day."

"Snow day?"

Indeed. It snowed on February 14, 1997, and the snow continued well into the next week. I overanalyzed the situation and realized how weird George would think I was for breaking into his locker and putting in dead flowers. The anxiety was unbearable. I prayed for a snowplow so I could retrieve the items. I prayed for a time machine. I prayed for death.

It was the end of the day on February 19th when I received a phone call.

"Hello, Stephanie?"

"Yes?"

"Hi, this is Dawn. Um, I didn't see you at school today."

"We had school today?"

My mom, on wiretap duty in the other room, replied, "Is still too snowy. I don't vant no bus getting in an accident and killing my only child. I only have von, you know-"

"Am I in trouble?" I asked. I didn't know anyone named Dawn so I assumed she was school administration.

"No. Uh, I was looking for you because you put flowers in my locker."

I mentally rejoiced. Someone else found the flowers. I was saved!

"Oh, I'm sorry about that. You can throw them out. It was a mistake."

"No, I saw that they were for George. He has the locker next to mine so I gave them to him. I thought you should know they smelled real bad."

Word about the incident circulated around school. Apparently, the flowers didn't only die, they also became putrid. Their mildewy goo secreted onto the bear, the note, and poor Dawn's sheet music. Kiara was all too happy to pitch in with a description of her walking in on me as I was "ritually cleansing the bear" as part of a Wiccan ritual to force George to love me.

Not only did George never speak to or look at me again, but Tiffany pretended not to know me either.

* * *

I was mortified, and I berated myself for falling for someone so easily. A week later, I was at church, licking my wounds and doing odd jobs to earn credits so I could go to summer camp for free. I was washing dishes and cleaning up after the Youth Group when I started going over a mantra in my head.

Remember, Stephanie, I told myself. School, work, art, eat, church, sleep, repeat. Wait, who's that guy? Oh my gosh, is he coming over here? No! Stop it! School, work, art, eat, church, blue eye, green eye, what? He has two different colored eyes?

"Hi," said the guy with the two different colored eyes. He was wearing a hemp necklace with a silver flower on it. He donned a faded Sublime T-shirt and single gold earring. He had a goatee and long dirty blond hair tied back into a ponytail.

"Hello," I said, voice cracking.

He looks like Jesus, I thought. You can't like Jesus more than a friend. That's probably a sin.

"Do you have any more chips?" he asked.

I did, under the counter. His name was John and I was able to buy his love with a stale bag of LAY'S® Classic Potato Chips.

He complimented my shirt, which had a picture of an egg with arms and legs, the image of Fantastic Dizzy, an obscure video game character I liked. He couldn't believe I'd designed the shirt myself, and he asked to see my sketchbook. I didn't know it at the time, but he was to become my real high school sweetheart, my first love, and my first of many things.

John was two years older than I was so we had no classes together. At first, I only saw him on Wednesday nights at Youth Group. After he bought a rusted old car for $500, I got to see him on weekends and we officially started going steady. John was a man of few words. At that point in my life, there were so many words and opinions coming at me from all directions, fewer words meant a lot to me. John was cute and, most importantly, laid back. He didn't like to argue. He had a sleepy look and a half-smile on his face at all times. We could talk about nothing and it was fine.

He took interest in my art. He had no drawing ability himself, but he was handy. He was learning to be an electrician with his father, John Sr., and he taught me how to make crazy lamps and basic gadgets. It was easy to be with him, and his mom and dad liked me.

I was worried at first that Anyu would have a problem with my dating. Of all of the things she was overprotective about, it turned out dating was not one of them. As long as she got to meet the guy beforehand and we didn't do anything death-defying like go near water, fire, or zoo animals, she was fine with me going on dates.

Her only criticism of John?

"Vhy you date such feminine men? He doesn't look like a guy dat vould have chest hair you can really grab onto."

The image of my mother grabbing onto Tom Selleck's chest hair made me want to barf. But in a strange way, I took her lack of major protest as a compliment. To her, female value was determined by how many male suitors were knocking on The Kapu to deliver flowers. It was gross to talk about which kind of men we each liked, I thought, but maybe in this one weird way, Anyu and I were bonding.

CHAPTER 24: THE PROM

JOHN AND I had been going out for an entire year. He was a senior, I was a sophomore, and it was obvious we'd go to the prom together because we were a serious couple. The prom was the talk of the school, but for many students, it posed an economic challenge. The tickets were expensive, as were limos, flowers, and of course, fancy tuxes and dresses. Luckily for me, in addition to being the queen of savings, my aunt Neni was also a great seamstress so I wasn't too worried about it.

I should have been more worried.

I'd grown to my full height of five foot ten, more than six feet tall with heels on, and I was having a difficult time finding a dress that reached my ankles. Neni was convinced that I was still growing, so she wanted me to size up. We had several months before the prom. In her opinion, I might grow another five, ten, twenty inches and go from an A-cup to a DDD. I wasn't crazy about the thought of getting any taller, but since I was secretly hoping that some more impressive boobs would eventually appear, I agreed. She assured me that she'd alter the dress before the prom to ensure I had a perfect fit.

I tried on about 500 fuchsia-sequin-encrusted, lace-imbued dresses before I found my little black dress. It was simple, with fantastic rhinestone spaghetti straps. Most importantly, it was on clearance for $19.95. I was proud of this discount find and paid for the dress myself with the money I'd earned from Slomin's Shield.

I'd forgotten that my aunt's seamstressing work was largely focused on couch cushions, not dresses. That spring, business had been so crazy she hadn't had time to deal with my gown. Before we knew it, the prom was upon us, and my dress was not altered. And my usual go-to hair and makeup expert, Erin, was on her honeymoon with her husband.

My other cousin, Irina, a crunchy granola, natural beauty kind of girl, was sure we could make it work.

"I read that Hollywood stars glue themselves into their dresses before their award shows," she said.

"Really?" I asked. That sounded like a good idea.

The night of the prom, Neni and Irina came over to help me get ready. I was hanging out of my dress. The boobs never came in, so whenever I bent over, whatever little cleavage I had poured over the top. Irina attempted to Krazy Glue the dress onto my bosom. It left a huge white stain on the front of the black dress.

"My dress doesn't fit and it's ruined. My life is over!" I wailed.

"No problem," Neni said. "Ve'll fix it."

I looked over at Nagymama and Anyu for guidance. Anyu stood there, said nothing, and frowned. Nagymama was more worried about my eating dinner, which consisted of a huge bowl of lecsó, a dish made of stewed peppers, tomatoes, and rice. It's a simple, tasty dish, but like all our food, Nagymama cooked it for hours until it most closely resembled burning sulfur.

Throughout my life, when I'd visualized getting ready for the prom, I'd pictured that scene where all the mice delicately construct Cinderella's dress. I'd never imagined my cousin styling my hair with an '80s crimper while my aunt colored my boob in with a Sharpie marker and Nagymama spooned burning awful into my mouth.

"Nagymama, you're going to ruin her lipstick!" Irina shouted.

"She need to eat. And you making her look like a whore," Nagymama said.

"You're gonna poke her eye out vith dat eyeliner!" Anyu yelled.

"Stephie, you should get a better push-up bra next time," Neni added. "Guess dah boobs are not coming."

Irina held up a mirror, and I shrieked.

As a result of my cousin being ten years my senior, her sensibilities for hair styling fell into the crimped, poofy, poodle-y camp. Although this may have been a great look in the '80s, the year was 1998. My eyeliner looked less "smoky" and more "like an actual raccoon." My chest was red from the Krazy Glue chemical burn, and I had a big hard shiny spot in the center of my dress. My dress was being held together with pins that Neni had haphazardly placed all over and the fabulous rhinestones had started to fall out of the spaghetti straps.

It was at that exact moment John arrived at the door.

Since we'd begun dating, I'd tried to shelter John from the Yuhas family drama. He'd heard many of the stories, but it wasn't until he stood there witnessing it for himself that I saw the harsh reality taking hold in his brain. A 500-year-old babushka lady was grabbing him by his tuxedo buttons, pulling him inside a strange, smelly shack, forcing him to sit at a sticky kitchen table, and pushing a bowl of molten peppers on him. He smiled politely, declined, and informed us the limo was waiting outside.

"Here, I got you this." He put a beautiful glittery corsage of white roses on my wrist.

I smiled. For a moment, I felt pretty, and everything else fell into the background.

Irina asked, "Where's the boutonniere?"

"What's a boutonniere?" I asked, looking at John, who shrugged.

In the distance, I heard a microwave beeping, but I thought nothing of it.

Irina was exasperated. "You moron! You're supposed to buy your date a flower that matches your corsage so people know you're together!"

I'd never been to the prom before or witnessed anyone else's prom-goings. I had no idea that this was a custom.

"No problem," Neni said. "Ve'll improvise." She pulled the corsage off my wrist, grabbed a kitchen knife, and started hacking it to pieces.

Meanwhile, Nagymama walked over to my date with a glass of orange juice. "Nice boy," she said, as she patted him on the butt.

John shifted uncomfortably and took a sip.

"Anyu!" I said. "Nagymama is touching John inappropriately!"

He looked over at me. "No, it's okay, she's fine...but..." He paused for a second, staring down at the juice, not wanting to offend. He then realized Nagymama could not understand much English, and he may as well be honest. "I can't finish this."

He handed me the cup of steaming orange juice. So afraid was Nagymama of cold that she warmed up the orange juice in the microwave, transforming concentrate into battery acid.

"Oh, God. Forget it. We're leaving."

I threw the juice in the sink, grabbed John's hand, and ran out the door with Neni chasing after us.

"Vait, vait! Dah flowers!" Neni grabbed John and struggled to pin the hacked-apart corsage remnants onto his lapel. I pulled the tattered pieces of the corsage back on my wrist and started heading towards the gate.

Anyu stopped us. "Vait! Von last ting! Let me get a picture of the happy couple!"

Caption not necessary.

I grabbed John and ran to the limo as fast as my high-heeled shoes would carry me. But I was stopped by The Kapu.

As I waited for Nagymama to come out with her Kapu key, my entire prom party watched from the limousine. I was anxious; I was sure that the sight of two young adults in formal wear getting locked behind a fence by a four-foot-tall woman wearing papucs and a babushka would be captured on everyone's camera.

"You vasted good orange chooce," she said to John, closing The Kapu behind her. She scowled at him. I knew he would be added to her list of nightly mutterings.

*   *   *

We desperately crawled into the limo and I prepared myself for the onslaught of teasing. However, I found our prom party rummaging through a mini fridge and inspecting some sort of liquid in a glass decanter. John's friend Anthony whispered, "Yo, I think they have booze on this bus!"

I was thrilled, not about the liquor, but about the fact that no one but John had witnessed my family debacle. My joy subsided when Crystal said, "Whoa. What smells like dirty diapers?"

"We live in New Jersey. *Everything* smells like dirty diapers," I retorted.

Everyone laughed, attention turned back to the booze, which Anthony was proudly pouring into glasses he'd found in the limo cup holders. But I knew the truth. It was the lecsó. The stench of peppers cooked for ten thousand years combined with Nagymama's body odor covered every single inch of my being and John's tux, too.

John looked like he was going to reach for the decanter but stopped himself. I smiled at him. We'd promised each other we'd abstain from drinking until we were 21 years old and sex until we were married. I felt comfort in knowing there was someone wholesome by my side.

After a few more blocks of driving around in a limo, we arrived at the prom, which took place at a Greek restaurant with floor-to-ceiling mirrors sandblasted with screaming swans. As I was sarcastically remarking about a statue of a baby cherub peeing into a fountain, my ex-boyfriend Jamar, the one who'd exposed his penis to me, came into my line of vision. He was with his entourage, feeding a pig in a blanket to his date, oblivious to my arrival. That is, until his moron best friend Chip, a squat little man with a voice reminiscent of Nelson from *The Simpsons*, stopped and pointed his finger at me.

"Why are you here, Step-on-me You-ass?" Chip snorted.

"I'm sorry," I said reflexively but then caught myself.

Why was I about to apologize for being a sophomore invited to a Senior Prom? I'd done nothing wrong. It then occurred to me that all of the prom-goers except for me would be graduating in a week and I would never have to deal with them again.

"What did you call me?" I walked menacingly toward Chip.

Crystal trailed closely behind me, aware this was not going to end well.

Chip continued his teasing. "You heard me, Step-on-me You-ass!"

I did as he told me to do: I placed one high-heeled foot directly on him and stomped down as hard as I could.

Chip called out in pain and retreated to the back of his group. Surprisingly enough, Jamar laughed at this. He shook his head, told Chip to stop being an asshole, and ushered his group along.

There was no other reaction, no big revenge my family had warned me about provoking. In fact, it seemed I'd earned some respect.

Crystal shook her head, also laughing. "Looks like you're finally growing some balls, Steph. Way to stand up for your woman, John."

"What?" John said. He and Anthony hadn't seen any of the fight; they were busy playing with the stream emanating from the cherub penis fountain.

Inside the ballroom, John sat down next to me and immediately started devouring his dinner roll. I was worried he was mad about the Chip incident, but instead he complained about his grocery store job and asked if I wanted my bread. I couldn't get John to accompany me on the dance floor because he was too shy. The rest of my group wanted to dance, so I joined them. I was relieved when some early '90s techno song came on. We danced for two or three songs.

For a moment, I forgot myself, until the heat of the dance floor and the exertion of dancing pushed the power of Krazy Glue past its natural limits and my oversized dress fell down.

It was only for a split second, but that second was long enough for everyone to see *everything*.

Anthony laughed. "Guess you can lose that abstinence ring now since we've all seen your boobies. Prom night! Prom night!"

I would have given him a good punch in the arm, but dinner had arrived, and my date was asleep at the table.

CHAPTER 25: THE SHOWDOWN

SOMEONE HAD CONVINCED my mother that the extra-curricular activities, schoolwork, and part-time job I was holding down constituted a complex lie. I'm not sure if it was *20/20*, someone at church, my conspiracy theorist Aunt Neni, or some combination of the three. Anyu believed that I was secretly smoking marijuana and going to raves in the forest where hundreds of teens would be having unprotected group sex to the light of glow sticks.

It never occurred to me to do any of those things. I was getting straight A's, I wasn't coming home smelling any weirder than normal, and much to the dismay of my hormonal, meat-eating boyfriend, and I was a still a Christian Vegetarian Virgin.

It was fall of my junior year. I'd called Anyu earlier that afternoon to tell her I'd be staying late at school to see John's little brother play in the homecoming football game. Maybe she knew how much I detested sports and assumed she'd finally caught me in a lie. Watching sports felt like a normal American thing to do, and I clutched tightly to anything even remotely normal as often as I could.

Mostly, though, I wanted to hang out and eat junk food in the bleachers with John and his mom, Lily. John had graduated from high school the previous spring and was still living at home and working at ShopRite. We'd had a great summer together, and now that I was back in school, I missed spending time with him. Lily and I had also become good friends. I saw her as a second mother, a bit on the hippie-dippy side, but nurturing in ways my own mother could not be. We sat happily in the bleachers, eating, laughing, and not paying any attention to the game.

I didn't see my mother's car until it was too late. Her mustard-colored Dodge Aspen station wagon peeled into the loading zone. Like some kind of stunt driver in an action movie, she parked diagonally across the space next to the field and adjacent to the bleachers.

Anyu jumped out of her car and ran out onto the football field. "My daughter, my daughter! Has anyvon seen my daughter?" she frantically screamed.

Someone a few seats behind us laughed. "Man, I feel sorry for whoever has *that* crazy-assed mom."

John's mouth dropped, as did mine. I wondered why this was happening. What had I done to deserve this? What could I do to make it stop? Should I wave, knowing that would call attention to me? Should I go down there and get her? Should I...run?

As I went over the possible scenarios in my head, a familiar patch of red hair entered the field. I looked around our seats. John was still sitting beside me, but somehow, without my noticing, Lily had left her seat. She'd marched onto the field and was heading straight for Anyu.

Was this better? Was this way worse? I sat, frozen.

"What the hell are you doing?" Lily yelled. "You're humiliating your daughter in public for no reason, you psychopath!"

"Crap," John said, aware that his mother was also now humiliating me in public.

"She needs to come home right now!" yelled Anyu, loud enough for all 500 of my classmates to hear.

"Why? What is so important that you need to scream that on a football field?"

It dawned on me that she might be panicking due to an emergency. What if the house had burned down? What if Nagymama was doing death defying chores again and had fallen off the roof? What if my cousins had been kidnapped?

"She needs to come home because. . . I'm her mother and I think she should?"

Her words hit me hard. There *was* no good reason, I realized. I was trying to mimic an American teenager, and she was trying to mimic a concerned mother, but we were both lost in translation.

I'd always tried to give my mother the benefit of the doubt, to cut her slack in the face of our situation at home. I wasn't perfect, but I tried to be the best student, the best daughter, and the best Christian I possibly could be. And yet, she didn't trust me.

Whenever any outside force—Nagymama, Neni, or the news— implied that children were misbehaving, getting injured, or going missing, she'd instantly project that thought onto me and adjust her parenting style. None of her punishments were based on her own convictions or my actions. I could never consistently please her because what she wanted from me was always changing.

Down on the field, Lily was backing away slowly to lure Anyu into a more isolated part of the parking lot near her station wagon. I ran down the bleachers as quickly as I could. John, normally much faster than me, had trouble keeping up.

Clearly I was wild woman.

By the time I ran over to them, Lily and Anyu were loudly screaming profanities at each other as they debated what constituted appropriate public behavior. I was waiting for one of them to throw a punch. Anyu spotted me.

"Let's go." She grabbed me and tried to push me into the car, but I didn't budge.

"Did I do something wrong?" I asked.

"I don't like it. I don't like it. Clubs. Church. Art. It all bullshit. You bullshitting me."

"I don't understand," I said. "What are you specifically freaking out about?"

"Why don't you pay attention to your daughter?" Lily asked. "Come to her shows if you don't believe her. Chaperone Youth Group. Do something as her mother. Get a job so you can help the girl go to college."

"I didn't go to no stupid college."

"Aren't we supposed to want better lives for our children?"

"You think you're her mother? Even your kids are too stupid to go to college! You don't know half of the bullshit I deal vith!"

"Bullshit? I work for a living. What do you do? I make home-cooked meals, not serve McDonald's every day. We have a mattress for Stephanie to sleep on and a place where she can work on her projects. We have a *door* on our *bathroom*!"

"Vell, I'm a student!" Anyu lied.

I shook my head, having heard her use this line before to explain why she hadn't worked since 1987, a mystery I don't understand to this day.

"Stephie, come on, let's go."

John looked at me. "Do you want to go with your mom?"

"No," I said. How I felt whenever I was around John and Lily compared to how I felt around my own family made the decision crystal clear. "I don't."

"Okay," said Lily. "She's never coming home with you again. If you want her, go ahead and call Child Protective Services. They can look at your house and my house and see who's better equipped to nurture the mind, body, and soul of a 16-year-old girl."

My mother was stunned into silence, though Lily was making an empty threat. Any professional agency would have made me go home with my own mother. But Anyu was terrified of the authorities. So she got in her car, slammed the door, and drove away.

I never lived with Anyu or Nagymama again.

The rest of the game was a blur, and none of us watched it. We sat in that parking lot—Lily, John, and I—a new family unit. I kept replaying the incident and my reaction to it. My primary feeling was immense relief washing over me, bringing tears to my eyes.

As much as I knew this life change was for the best, I realized it was a mixed blessing for Anyu. She worried so excessively about the need to care for me that knowing she no longer had to was probably a relief for her as well, I imagined. At the same time, she was now alone with Nagymama. The thought of them living in that house without their rituals of overprotection to unite them gave me chills. These two paranoid women who were already getting on each other's last nerves now had to spend the rest of their lives together, unless either of them chose to change.

John squeezed my hand. I'd nearly forgotten he was there. John and Lily had been talking to me, asking me questions, for I don't know how long. Ten seconds? Ten minutes?

"Are you okay?" Lily asked.

I smiled at them. For the first time that I could remember, I was.

CHAPTER 26: CORRUPTION

"I KNOW YOU'VE BEEN watching your weight so I made these brownies with spinach and Swiss chard," Lily said, waving a tray of baked goods at me. "Thirty percent less fat!"

"So I can eat thirty percent more of them, right? Ha, ha!" I said, grabbing a brownie and taking a bite. The texture was odd, but it was still chocolate, which seemed to make everything better. I'd been stressing about my senior show, my family, and the usual high school drama.

"See, I knew I always wanted a daughter," Lily replied with a wink.

"Wanna rent a movie tonight, babe?" John asked, placing his arm around me. "Anthony's working at the video store. He'll probably be able to hook us up with a new release for free."

"Okay, but I have to finish this sketch project and some reading for AP English. I wish I didn't take these stupid AP classes."

Life was not as utopian as the picture Lily had painted to my mother, but overall I was happy. The house was home to Lily and husband, John Sr., my boyfriend John (Jr.), his two brothers, one dog (that terrified me), three cats (that terrified me more), and a rotating cast of vagabonds like me that the family allowed to couch surf from time to time. John had a bit of a hoarding problem, so I had to share space with his treasures, which included childhood toys, movie stubs, and straw wrappers from our first date. Even with these moving pieces, it was quieter and roomier than the home I'd grown up in. Every night, this eclectic family gathered around the dining room table to break bread and share stories. It was like a hippie version of a Norman Rockwell painting.

Sure, the house smelled of smoke, but it was a step up from feces, body odor, and mold like my house. They had a DVD player and a VCR, cable television, two bathrooms (with doors), a working washing machine, and a workbench where we could create awesome things. I

didn't know where all the booze bottles were coming from, but I knew
how to turn them into art. We smashed tiles out back and created large
mosaics. We made a lot of palm tree lamps and talked about moving to
paradise someday.

We'd polished off nearly all the brownies when my lips and tongue
started to go numb.

"You guys," I managed to say, worried I was having an allergic
reaction. "Somethin wron. My tongue is tinglingngngn?"

Lily put a reassuring hand on my shoulder. "It's just a little pot
brownie, sweetie. You need to relax. You're only young once."

"Wha the heck? You tryn ta poison me?"

I was mad. Aside from my accidental ingestion of Black Russians at
Olga and Dimitri's house as a child, I never drank alcohol, let alone took
recreational drugs. What kind of mother would drug her son's
girlfriend with the promise of health food?

"Yeah," John added. "You got into college already! The rest of the
year doesn't matter, as long as you get good enough grades to walk."

"You're all mean," I said. Why was the pot making me feel like a
little kid again? Was this good or really bad? Was I being a stick-in-
the-mud and too strict for nothing? What was better—oppressively
protective love or free and potentially dangerous love? I had no idea
what was right or wrong at that point.

I'd been realizing, slowly, that John wasn't the innocent I'd thought
he was. A few weeks earlier, he'd gotten fired from his grocery store job
for stealing some baked cheese crackers and a Barbie Doll. He'd been
forced to spend the night in jail, gotten banned from ShopRite for life,
and now had a record. I felt terrible because he was stealing those
items as gifts for me. John did everything in his power to make me
happy. I assumed this was just another dumb, illegal attempt at love.

But didn't he know me well enough to know I wouldn't want to
take drugs in the middle of a million important school projects? I
wanted to be perfect. I wanted to learn as much as possible. Sure, I
thought in my haze, it sucked that I was taking advanced classes and
doing a ton of extra-curricular activities and I still couldn't make my
mother proud of me. It sucked that my pastor criticized me for being
too smart, asking too many questions, and not having enough blind
faith. It sucked that I ate a healthy vegetarian diet, exercised, and

didn't have sex but still looked three months pregnant. And yeah, maybe it sucked that although I was a (now questioning) Christian Vegetarian Virgin, people still called me a slut because I lived with my boyfriend. Wait. It all totally sucked.

So I let go. For that moment, stoned out of my mind, I allowed myself to be a dumbass teenager.

Gee, if there were only some signs that my boyfriend was a pothead.

Looking back on it, a lot of what I did and experienced that fateful year of 2000 was questionable. I tried pot again and alcohol, too, by choice. We got a bunch of *Weird New Jersey* magazines and trespassed on supposedly haunted but definitely private property. And after a bit of convincing, I lost my virginity to a novelty glow-in-the-dark condom, in a single bed, in a room filled with garbage. After the awkward deed was done, John rolled over, stole the paper-thin blanket, and fell right asleep.

John snored as loud as Nagymama. The bed was smaller than the piece of upholstery foam I was used to sleeping on and not very nice. Instead of being surrounded by chairs, I was pressed up against a cold wall and a rattling headboard covered in tiny alcohol bottles and broken old Happy Meal toys. Lying there naked and freezing, too afraid to inconvenience John by asking for more of the blanket, I missed the shoelaces that kept the blanket in place at my old house. I pulled a velvet black light unicorn poster off of the wall and draped it over myself. I wondered why no one told me that becoming an adult would be so uncomfortable.

A month before my high school graduation, John asked if I would be willing to add a third person to our relationship. He confessed that he'd been cheating on me with a stripper but promised me we could all be together if I just agreed to this new, improved liaison. To me, this was too much freedom.

I ran through piles of trash, past the cats, dog, and vagabonds, right to my cousin Erin, hoping she would have a solution. It was hard to face her, knowing that I'd lost my faith and my virginity. She had waited until marriage to have sex with her husband. I was too ashamed to tell her the truth about my own choices.

She and her husband took me in. She washed the smoke smell out of my clothing and taught me how to use the stove. She made sure my financial aid paperwork was in order for college. For one short month, she was my mother, and she was great at it.

Erin also tried to keep my mind off of John, but I couldn't stop myself from continuing to visit his house. I was not there to win him back; I was still very close with Lily and she was in trouble. She'd found out that her husband had been cheating on her and she'd kicked him out. With John Sr. gone, her wild teenage sons and their friends were breaking and stealing everything. Her home had turned into a drug den and she didn't know how to fix it. I was torn between three mothers.

Because I was out late most nights helping Lily, Erin assumed I was up to no good and started leaving religious pamphlets on my bed. I felt a crushing judgment come down on me. I could not live in another house of eggshells.

My brain told me to stay with Erin but my heart told me to move back in with Lily. We needed each other. We'd both been betrayed by a John. She was the only one who didn't judge me, was proud of me, and knew me for exactly who I was. Not the fragile little girl who needed to be protected. Not the fake veil of virginal perfection. Just me.

The night before I left for college, Lily and I sat on her stoop, arms circled around each other. "I'm so happy he cheated on you now because he would have cheated on you later," she said, referring to John. "He's just like his father. And what if he'd gotten you pregnant, like my John did? At least now you have your whole life ahead of you. Promise me that you will never let another person hold you back."

I promised her.

CHAPTER 27: PHILADELPHIA

MY MATRICULATION into University of the Arts was now underway, and I was in my aunt's huge green van she used for her upholstery business, driving from Piscataway to what would be my home from this point forward: Philadelphia.

I knew this wasn't going to be a typical college experience where I'd be bringing laundry home and mooching home-cooked meals every other weekend. I never had those things to begin with. Even though Anyu and I had drawn a tenuous truce and tensions had cooled to a simmer, I knew this was going to be a true goodbye. A casting off of the awkward and isolating past I'd come to know as the default way of life. I was going to be a part of that poster that had hung on my wall for the last four years. I could tell from the fake poster eyes that every person was going to be like me, an independent artist, and I'd finally be accepted.

Despite my aunt's extremely hazardous 35-mile-per-hour driving down I-95, despite Anyu and Neni bickering over whether we were driving too fast or too slow, despite frequent stops to consult the map and dump out pee from the McDonald's Halloween Bucket, the thought of the community I was about to join kept a smile on my face the whole ride down to Philadelphia. I couldn't stop grinning at my brand new dorm keys. They were held together with a handmade keychain John had given me before I left, a parting gift, in hopes we could still be friends. The keychain was a silver fortune cookie, with a tiny message poking out of it: "Become Who You Are."

A week earlier, I'd pulled out one last surge of strength to make a final offering to Anyu. I'd been worried that my move to another state would make her feel abandoned, though I'd also been terrified that shifting even slightly back to my own life would feel horribly stressful and smothering.

"Anyu?" I'd said, hoping for a real answer instead of a guilt trip. "Are you sure you're OK? I can take the train home on weekends, if you want?"

"No," she said, resignation in her voice. "It's better that you stay in Philadelphia. Don't come home."

This meant, "Don't come home at all, not even for Christmas or summer." The idea of me dying while taking the train back home frightened her. She had no interest in me coming home unless it was with a man—preferably a rich husband who could finally buy the family the bi-level they'd always wanted.

I knew a part of her wanted to tell me to come back to help her, both to provide a buffer between herself and Nagymama and to give her something else to occupy her thoughts. Somewhere inside me, I understood that allowing me to exit without drama or conflict or guilt was noble and selfless on her part. But I was definitely not about to force the issue. I didn't want to fall into the Stockholm syndrome trap she'd fallen into with Nagymama. Instead of being sad, I'd been relieved. I was free.

When we reached Philadelphia, Anyu and Neni initiated the Family Panic I'd learned to tune out by now. They were so busy telling me to be careful crossing the street and not to bring homeless cats or people back to my dorm they didn't even seem to notice the impressive skyline growing ever closer, the prime real estate of the University's campus, smack dab in the center of the city's Avenue of the Arts, or the cultural, historical, and architectural splendor of this new world surrounding us. America had been founded here. As an immigrant family, I thought they'd be more excited.

I was drinking it all in as we unpacked the contents of the van into the dorm hallway. I couldn't wait to make new friends. To wake up and walk to class on my own timeframe, without Nagymama following me to the building to make sure I hadn't been stolen. To see which restaurants would become my go-tos. To meet my first-ever artistic roommate and see what we had in common. To be able to take a long shower if I were so inclined. To finally dye my hair red.

We loaded the last box into the dorm. There was an awkward silence for the first time that trip.

"Well, I guess you better go unpack!" said Neni.

"Do you want a glass or water or something?" I asked.

Nagymama had trained me well in the art of offering people water so they didn't mutter about my rudeness for the next thirty years. I even would have microwaved it for them if they'd wanted me to.

"No, no, we'd better go. Gonna be dark soon," Anyu said forebodingly.

"Okay, well, um, thanks, then, for, um, helping. With everything," I said.

Suddenly, Neni hugged me. It occurred to me that it wasn't awkward for the normal reason it is with college students, where both parties are thinking, "What does this mean for our relationship now that we're both adults?" It was awkward because none of us had actually hugged before. We were not a sentimental family. (Nagymama and I hadn't even said goodbye. Two years earlier, when I'd moved out, Anyu had lied and told her I'd gotten married. Nagymama didn't worry about me anymore because to her, I was some man's problem now.)

Out of the corner of my eye, I could see Anyu observing my hug with Neni. Anyu tilted her head ever so slightly, like an alien watching a human interaction for the first time.

Neni stepped away and I offered my open arms to Anyu. She walked hesitantly, shoulder first, into me, like a football player moving toward a tackling dummy in slow motion. She winced at this partial, weak hug, as if this gesture would cause her bones to shatter like a fake Howard Johnson's crystal glass. It was the kind of hug I could only reciprocate with a "there, there" pity pat.

The elevator door opened. My family shuffled in.

I wondered if I should say, "I love you," like we did at John's house. But we were not a family who said, "I love you," not at any point in my eighteen years of life.

"Bye," I said.

Anyu waved half-heartedly.

The elevator doors closed. It dawned on me that the only way my mother and I could start a real relationship with each other was to support each other from a distance. To paraphrase Princess Leia and the band 38 Special, the tighter you grip the things you love, the more those things will slip through your fingers. This was the start of our new challenge, to hold each other loosely.

Alone in the hallway, surrounded by a sea of boxes, I looked down at the set of keys in my hand. No one in Philadelphia knew about my accent or my stutter, I reminded myself. They hadn't seen the patched-up sweatpants or smelled the rancid lecso. Art school was giving me a blank canvas, in more ways than one.

I put the keys into the lock and clumsily jiggled the doorknob. I took a deep breath as I stepped into my dorm room and my new life. What happened from here on out, I thought, was up to me.

ACKNOWLEDGMENTS

THANK YOU to my entire Booktrope family, especially Andy Roberts, Ken Shear, Katherine Sears, and Jesse James Freeman, for taking the leap of faith and publishing my first book, instead of throwing it into the big shedder where all manuscripts go to die. Publishing companies have those now, right? Or are they still using firey pits?

Thank you to my editor, Kathy Harding, for turning what was a bunch of blog entries filled with ads for zit cream into a real book. Thank you to Steve Luna and DS George-Jones for the editing tips that turned into therapy sessions. I especially appreciate that neither of you is a licensed therapist so you cannot bill me $400 per hour. Please enjoy the basket of cigarettes and coffee. That is how authors are usually paid, correct?

Thanks to Gabrielle Roman for fixing all of my typos, especially the pages and pages of "All work and no DORITOS® makes Steph a dull girl." I don't think we're licensed to use DORITOS® in this book. So I should probably stop saying DORITOS®. Thank you to Victoria Wolffe for laying out this book so I didn't have to spend 30 consecutive days uttering profanities at Adobe InDesign.

Thank you to Luanne Brown for taking on the bottomless pit of despair that is book marketing. I look forward to hearing your screams, as long as you can put them into 140-character blurbs or accompany them with some sort of cat meme. Thank you to Lowell Boston for the motivation, Jeremy Doe for featuring the animation that inspired this book on YouTube, and to Fred Seibert and Eric Homan for putting the same animation on Nicktoons. Nagymama finally got her 15 minutes of fame.

Thank you to my stylist, Sara Green, and my photographer, Rachel Troche, for making me look nice on this book cover. For the sake of honesty, I will now include a photo of what I normally look like. I still don't know why this was rejected by our marketing team.

Drink me in, boys.

Thank you to my family for making me who I am today, in the most entertaining fashion possible. I appreciate the perspective you've given me and the time you've dedicated to me, back then and even now.

Last but not least, thank you to my business partner and husband, Matt Conant. You can pick your friends, you can pick your nose, and for whatever reason, you picked our dysfunctional but happy family.

MORE GREAT READS
FROM BOOKTROPE

Bumbling into Body Hair – A Transsexual's Memoir by **Everett Maroon** (Memoir) A comical memoir about a klutz's sex change, showing how a sense of humor—and true love—can triumph over hair disasters, and even the most crippling self-doubt.

Dizzy in Karachi by **Maliha Masood** (Memoir) An intimate account of the experience of living, working and traveling within a country teeming with contradictions.

Holding True by **Emily Dietrich** (Contemporary Fiction / Coming of Age) Born in the hopeful energy of the civil rights movement, Martie struggles to live out the values she inherited by founding the Copper Hill commune, with tragic results.

Under the Squatting Eagle by **Dennis Fishel** (Biographical Fiction) Dennison McDowell decides higher education is just too much work and puts the books down in favor of a job as a letter carrier with the US Postal Service.

Sweet Song by **Terry Persun** (Historical Fiction) This tale of a mixed-race man passing as white in post-Civil-War America speaks from the heart about where we've come from and who we are.

Summer Melody by **Toddie Downs** (Women's Fiction) In a town called Daedalus Falls, it's easy for the weight of wings to overwhelm. But in the summer of 1992, three generations of women in the Stanton family realize untapped strengths that give them the power to soar.

Discover more books and learn about our
new approach to publishing at **booktrope.com**.

Made in the USA
San Bernardino, CA
08 August 2015